Beautiful Living

Elevate Every Room with Your Signature Style

VALERIE DARDEN

Founder of Brexton Cole Interiors

ROCK
POINT

To my amazing husband, Jonathan,
and my two sons, Cole and Brexton.

CONTENTS

INTRODUCTION 06

PART ONE 12
INDIVIDUAL ROOMS

PERFECT PASSAGE 14
The Entryway

COMMUNAL LOUNGES 28
The Living Room and Family Room

A HOME'S HEART 48
The Kitchen

GATHERING TABLE 60
The Dining Room

DREAM OASIS 78
The Primary Bedroom

REJUVENATION ZONE 100
The Primary Bathroom

IMAGINATION STATION 112
The Kids' Rooms

THINKING SPACE 122
The Home Office

PART TWO 130
STYLE GUIDE

PART THREE 198
COMMON QUESTIONS

REFERENCES 216

ACKNOWLEDGMENTS 221

ABOUT THE AUTHOR 222

Introduction

I WAS DISCOVERING A NEW LIFE PASSION IN INTERIOR DESIGN. MY MOTHER TAUGHT ME EVERYTHING SHE KNEW.

I grew up in a small town in New Jersey, in a place where families stay for generations. My parents met in high school, got married, and eventually had me—their only child. I remember riding my bike to my friends' houses after school, playing kickball at the school playground until sunset, and participating in making floats for the town's Fourth of July parade every year, come rain or shine. As much as I enjoyed my time in New Jersey, by the time I entered high school, I knew that I wanted more. I wanted to see the world and find work in other places. Staying in my small hometown was simply not in the cards for me.

If you asked me twenty years ago what my future profession would be, I can say, with confidence, that I would *not* have said interior designer. Back in the (what seems like prehistoric) year of 2000, when I graduated high school, I thought I would be a soccer star of some sort. If not a soccer star, then something involving sports. A personal trainer maybe? Possibly a high-level soccer coach for an important team in Europe? Ah, the dreams of youth!

Fast-forward to the present day and none of my sports dreams came true. After playing soccer in college in 2004, I severely injured my knee, and my soccer career quickly came to an end. I decided to get out of sports altogether. (By 2004, the burnout from sports was real!) I had so many injuries and was exhausted overall. I forgot my soccer dreams and moved to Virginia in 2007.

Since then, I've worked in every field possible. I waited tables, became a teacher, dabbled in sales, worked as an office assistant, and landed in vocational counseling, which I enjoyed and stuck with for a while.

In the summer of 2012, I discovered Instagram. Like the rest of the world, I began posting photos of my daily life. I thought the app was fun and I loved posting photos with the early filters. By then, I was married to my amazing husband, Jonathan, and we had bought our first home in Virginia. Luckily for me, my mother has been a successful interior designer in New Jersey for thirty years. She obtained her degree in the arts in the 1970s and knew the design world like the back of her hand. After buying our first home, I called her daily for home décor tips. I wanted to know where to buy decent furniture, how to pick proper paint colors, and how to install wallpaper. I have always been very close to my mom, but looking back, I am sure I drove her insane!

Little by little our first house came together, and I certainly made mistakes through the process. For example, I painted our downstairs bathroom hot pink. I thought it would look cool with black accents such as a large baroque-style mirror. Thinking about it to this day gives my husband and me terrible shudders. It was more of a *shocking* pink instead of hot pink. I still see it in my design nightmares! *Awful*! Needless to say, that bathroom did not make it onto my initial Instagram feed. (Thank goodness!)

Along the way, I began taking photos of the decorating progress of my home and posting them to Instagram and even Facebook. With my mom's instruction, my eye for interior design greatly improved.

Slowly, my Instagram follower count grew, and I began to take more of an interest in interior design. By this time, many local followers were messaging me with home décor questions and the possibility of taking on projects in their homes. I happily agreed to client projects as a side job. I remember acting very confident in front of clients, but in reality, I was scared to death of making poor design decisions. After every client meeting, I would run to my car, call my mother, and ask her about a hundred questions.

During those first two years, I consulted my mother about everything. I was discovering a new life passion in interior design, and she passed on to me everything she knew. She taught me about architecture, how to use color, mix patterns, lay out rooms, accessorize, work with contractors, measure, and use computer design programs. I was basically her apprentice, and

I learned an abundance of precious information. During this time, we visited each other often. I will never forget how greatly valuable the in person instruction from my mother was.

By 2016, my mother's confidence in my design skills grew and she began asking me to help design rooms for her clients in New Jersey. Since we lived in different states, we were on the phone constantly. We worked over Zoom and sent about twenty-five emails a day to one another tweaking rooms, talking to contractors, and purchasing furniture.

By 2017, I felt confident enough to open my interior design business, Brexton Cole Interiors, named after my two sons (born in 2013 and 2017). Since then, Brexton Cole Interiors has taken off. More people began following the business's Instagram account. Many clients have requested to work with us in Virginia and out of state. We also began getting some great press with offers for freelance writing and social media consulting. The more I posted and wrote about interior design, the more I realized that this was my lifelong passion.

And the rest is history! After years of design client questions over social media, email, and in person, I decided to put together this book.

Since this book is a fun interior design cheat guide, I wrote it in three parts. The first part is broken down by individual rooms and showcased through photos of my house. The second part will give you important guides you need for designing your home with ease. The third part is a Q&A that answers all of my most asked questions. Come with me as I give you the interior design tips and tricks that you can use to make your home look incredible!

PART ONE

INDIVIDUAL ROOMS

COME ON IN! If you're looking to spice up your house, you have come to the right place. In this section, we will touch on making every room visually appealing so that you know the dos and don'ts of how to design every space. From your living space to your kids' rooms, you'll learn design tips that you can use to make the most beautiful living all on your own.

The room chapters are in order of how I think you should go about designing the various areas of your home. You'd be surprised at how much you can do to a space to make it look more elevated and suit your style. The best part of this book? You don't have to spend thousands to get your home looking how you want. Use my long-lasting tips to make your home something to show off and be proud of.

Perfect Passage

THE ENTRYWAY

THIS IS THE PERFECT SPACE TO "WOW" GUESTS UPON ARRIVAL.

Out of every room in the home, the entryway is often the last space my clients are interested in designing. Some may even use a side door, garage door, or mudroom to enter the home, but the same thing is true: it is often overlooked for spaces such as kitchens and living rooms, which I totally get! It's meant for just passing through, right? Well, here is the kicker: the entryway is the perfect space to "wow" guests upon arrival.

Entryways come in many shapes and sizes. Some come with large ceilings and sweeping staircases, others are narrow little rooms most often found in charming centuries-old homes, and some houses' entryways are only big enough to hold a welcome mat. But, no matter how they look, they serve the same purpose. Entryways set the tone for the rest of our home's aesthetic. They also are a place for organization and function.

Depending on the size of your entryway (and the size of your family), you need smart storage solutions. Custom storage units like built-in benches, console tables, and closets are great ideas. If your entryway is tiny, try to stay away from a massive built-in. Instead, go for pretty wall hooks or cute boxes.

Since my family is a family of four (my husband, Jonathan, my two boys, and myself), we did not need too much extra storage. The entryway in our current home is a larger space, where, off to the side, we have a standard closet for jackets, cardigans, boots, and hats. For the times we entertain guests, however, I bought a vintage coatrack online. Not only is it gorgeous, but it adds extra organization without taking up too much space.

I was excited to move into my new home because this was the first grand-style entryway I had ever owned. With this one, I wanted guests to have that "wow" moment. I also wanted a design that would remain in style for decades, otherwise known as "timeless." I accomplished that on the walls where I used the traditional Schumacher Hydrangea Drape Wallpaper. This stunning pattern was featured in the 1939 movie *Gone with the Wind*. I will never forget the scene when Vivien Leigh runs down the stairs at the Tara plantation home. The wallpaper is only in the background, but I fell in love with the pattern right then and there!

An antique console table fit this space perfectly. It was large enough to hold a small tray to drop off mail, extra change, and keys. I styled it with my favorite candles, fashion books, a table lamp for the evenings, and a tall mirror to add natural light.

While I love vintage patterns and furniture, I also enjoy adding modern touches. The mixture of traditional and modern décor creates a multilayered space. It also keeps the home from looking like your grandmother's house. The modern pieces are the AERIN Mill Cage Pendant in gold, a marble table, custom X benches in a funky pattern, abstract art, and a zebra-print rug. (Turn back to page 15 where you can see all these design elements.)

MIRRORS ADD NATURAL LIGHT AND HELP ROOMS APPEAR LARGER.

PRO TIP

I recommend hanging a mirror adjacent to a window if possible. Mirrors add natural light and help rooms appear larger. If there isn't a window, a mirror will still trick the eye into thinking the space is larger than it actually is.

Your entryway needs function, organization, and an overall peaceful vibe. My top five favorite décor items to add to an entryway are books, chic candles, unique matches, decorative trays, and picture frames and photos. If you have the space, a statement chandelier can make a huge difference style wise. If you have a window at the front of your home, hang the chandelier centered in the window.

Pictured opposite is an entryway in a historic house in Virginia built in the 1830s. They used a traditional-style cabinet table with a multitude of décor elements used to create an interesting entryway.

Here is an example of a medium-sized entryway that has all of the essentials a home would need. An ottoman comes in handy to take off shoes, set down items, etc. If you have a larger space to work with, invest in a storage bench. You can also place a basket next to the console table or chair; just make sure to keep your basket height shorter than your chair or bench.

Cabinet tables are another great way to add closed storage. You can put anything you want on them, such as candles, trays, a vase of flowers, among many more things. They work as tabletops for when you have your hands full while entering or exiting your home, and it provides the perfect opportunity to place a mirror above.

In the photo, the entryway is wallpapered. If you want to dabble in wallpaper, this is a great room to do so to accomplish that "wow" factor.

MUDROOMS

A mudroom is a space usually near a back or side entrance of the home where you can remove any muddy boots/shoes or jackets before entering the more formal spaces. Mudrooms give people a chance to remove any wet clothing and store dirty pet accessories or muddy footwear to avoid tracking water, dirt, and germs throughout the house.

A mudroom is a great space to add extra storage for outdoor clothing and shoes. It is also perfect if you lack storage in your entryway. Instead of cluttering the floor there, use the mudroom for items such as shoes, bags, and umbrellas.

Most homeowners pay around 10,000 to 16,000 American dollars to add a mudroom to the home. The benefit is that home additions such as this will typically net an increase of 50 to 80 percent in resale value. Mudrooms are common in new homes and desirable with resale of older homes. If you want or have a mudroom, make it functional with cubbies, shelves, or drawers for storage, seating for putting on and taking off shoes, and a durable nonslip mat or rug to keep the space as dry as possible. You can even make a small pet area for bathing or storing leashes and outdoor equipment, or a laundry room so that wet and dirty clothes don't have to be trekked through the house.

Communal Lounges

THE LIVING ROOM AND FAMILY ROOM

FAMILY ROOMS ARE FAMILY FRIENDLY AND COZY. LIVING ROOMS, ON THE OTHER HAND, ARE OFTEN MORE ELEVATED, FORMAL SPACES.

As interior designers, we often get asked, "What is the difference between the living and family rooms?" Family rooms are family friendly and cozy. It's a more casual everyday place to watch television and chill out. Living rooms, on the other hand, are known as more elevated, formal spaces. Some homeowners might even call their living rooms "formal rooms," as oftentimes large houses—especially the beautiful older homes—will have both a family and a living room. But those definitions are entirely objective. The true purpose of any family or living room relies heavily on the people who own the home.

In my house, the living room and family room are the same. Ours is an open space off of the kitchen. It's a place where we can formally entertain and take it easy on a Sunday afternoon. No matter what your situation is, I will share some tips to help you create the perfect living space.

The main goal for a designer is for a room to look coordinated without matching entirely. Living spaces that coordinate include several materials, prints, and textures that work together and appear cohesive. For my home, my go-to color is green, and you'll find it in nearly every room! (See the next page for a photo of my living space.) It's the color of my sofas, the paint on the walls, the wallpaper, and even the dishes. If you love a certain color, then I say roll with it. The important thing is to keep it cohesive. I also love to mix old and new pieces throughout my home for a modern, eclectic vibe.

Many homeowners feel they need to use the same two colors for the entire room to make it balanced. This is not right! It's best to vary how much color appears in each individual room. Having a color story throughout a room or home gives that consistency that you want. Just make sure the main color still shines.

Don't be afraid to mix patterns. For my original living room design, I bought a Scalamandre Tiger print pillow, dotted benches, and green patterned wallpaper. The patterns are totally different, but the overall tone of the room works. With all the greens and various brass, creamy, and black accessories dotted around, the room looks pulled together. (See Mixing Patterns on page 152 and Mixing Metals on page 164 in the Style Guide.)

MONOCHROME LIVING ROOM

Monochrome is a common theme people use for their living rooms. Although monochrome can often mean various shades of one color, we often think of it as black and white. If you also like this theme, to give the room some dimension, I suggest using different patterns and textures. What does that mean? Let me walk you through a detailed example.

One of my clients wanted a monochrome living room with a modern yet cozy feel. To accomplish this, I added two black bouclé chairs, a matte metal table, a wool rug with a chevron pattern, and monochrome throw pillows with different patterns. I also added a wooden chair for not only warmth but also extra seating. (Natural woods look pretty in most spaces.) All these pieces made the monochrome look come together in a way that was not too overwhelming and gave my clients what they wanted. (Pictured is a monochrome living room I created for a client.)

A SOFA IS THE MOST IMPORTANT PIECE OF FURNITURE IN THE LIVING SPACE.

PRO TIP

Because it's usually the largest item, a sofa is the most important piece of furniture in the living space. Some designers will avoid placing furniture against the wall, especially the sofa because it can make the middle of the room feel cavernous. However, if it's not practical, I like to use the 2:3 rule of design. (See on page 142 in the Style Guide.) The overall goal is to create a conversation area that works for you and your individual space.

Most interior designers will say that having a rug in the room is a great design element. It adds texture and color and softens the space (if you have hardwood floors). My first recommendation is to purchase a rug that matches the other elements in the room, such as the chairs and sofas. This will make for a cohesive design. (See page 158 in the Style Guide.)

Lighting is also important when creating a relaxing living space. One essential thing to remember is that every room needs two to three light sources. It's especially important to light the corners of the room. Proper lighting helps our mood tremendously while also making the room appear larger. Spread the light around the room at various heights (high, medium, and low) using a mix of table lamps, floor lamps, and wall sconces. (For more, see page 166 in the Style Guide.)

PRO TIP

The process of arranging lighting in a room is called "task lighting." Imagine yourself sitting down on your sofa to read a book: you need ample light to see the words on the page. An example of task lighting, in this case, would be a table lamp or floor lamp next to the sofa.

Choosing a paint color is a huge decision to make when it comes to creating the perfect mood of a room, so I've created an entire section on paint (page 186) in Part Two of this book. However, I will share some tips now as you go about designing your living space.

I recommend buying small sample pots instead of picking from paper paint swatches. In most cases, paint swatches are very small and make it difficult to read how the paint color will appear all over the room. Instead, add a fairly large two-coat sample directly on a white wall. Then test the colors over a period of time in the daylight and at nighttime to make sure it's the right color.

Once you've figured out your optimal paint color, artwork creates texture and gives character. We want our homes to feel like our personal sanctuary, a place that screams *us*. Whether you take the minimal approach or love the "more is more" style, the room should reflect you and how you live your life. So, what is my message here? Try to follow the design rules, but at the end of the day, do what you love!

A SPACE SHOULD HAVE A CURATED AND COLLECTED FEEL TO IT.

PRO TIP

You don't want a room to be overly matchy-matchy. A space should have a curated and collected feel to it. Look at any professionally designed room and you'll rarely see three of the same style table or a matching bedroom set. You want to mix furniture pieces, use different textures, and mix vintage and modern accessories. In my living space, only the couches and mirrors are pairs. Everything else, especially the décor, are individual pieces that work together to create that curated feel.

A Home's Heart

THE KITCHEN

The kitchen is where many of my clients become frazzled. I cannot blame them either because I became frazzled with my own kitchen renovations! Kitchen renovations can be a costly and lengthy process depending on the aesthetic and layout you're looking to achieve. As a result, many of us may visit showrooms and retailers to seek assistance.

The cold truth that not everyone in the industry talks about is that, in some cases, working with a retailer means you are dealing with someone who is not an actual designer. When you see the job title of "sales/design team associate," this could mean that the person is a salesperson first and a designer second. Frequently, these individuals have more experience in sales than they do in actual interior design.

I do not mean to shade these job titles and individuals; I'm just telling you to be wary. Is there an exception to this rule? Absolutely. My mother, for example, worked at Ethan Allen for many years as a "design consultant." She was a trained interior designer and had her college degree in the field, and she still does incredible design work today!

The truth of the matter is that you can get help designing your kitchen from various places, but you will get individualized attention when hiring your own designer. If you go to a showroom, you will only be offered the products in that particular store that the design consultant works in so they can earn commission. If you hire a designer, you will be able to source the best materials and appliances from anywhere.

So much time is spent in the kitchen, from entertaining guests to food prep to homework at the kitchen island. Kitchens are certainly one of, if not the, most utilized rooms in the house. My goal as a designer is to help my clients use their kitchens in a functional manner while maintaining the style of the space they are looking for. With that said, one of my first questions I ask a client is what kind of renovation they want. A "cosmetic" renovation, for instance, focuses on updating your kitchen without making any expensive structural changes. An example of a cosmetic change would be replacing the pendants, purchasing new cabinet knobs, or painting the kitchen walls. After that, partial renovation or full renovation involves demolition, plumbing, and wiring. Once you figure out what kind of renovation you are looking for then you can start making your budget.

Pictured is a space in my butler's kitchen. We installed a rack to hang frequently used items or items that take up too much space in a drawer or cabinet. The backsplash is the modern-style subway tile that is easy to clean and maintain.

AV DE PARIS

VOIE GEORGES POMPIDOU

AV MOZART CHAMP DE MARS

AV VICTOR HUGO

AV DES CHAMPS-ELYSEES

AVENUE GUSTAVE EIFFEL

AV DE L'OPERA

BD SAINT-GERMAIN

BOULEVARD PERIPHERIQUE

RUE LAFAYETTE

AV GEORGE

O D'ORS

BE REALISTIC ABOUT WHAT YOU ARE ABLE TO SPEND.

The main thing I make sure to tell my clients is that kitchens are expensive to renovate. Kitchens carry costly demands such as updating appliances, plumbing, and electric and mechanical issues. (This is often truc in the case of historical homes.)

Another reason is simply because of the cost of cabinets and countertops. Great cabinets can result in a big payoff in the long term. You can choose from styles of American, glass, melamine, thermofoil, louvered, and more. The same goes for countertops. But if you're using stone countertops and doing a full cabinet installation, it can cost a pretty penny.

I adore the look of marble countertops, but sadly, with our lifestyle and two kiddos, it would not work in our home. We could have chosen marble and sealed it right away, but instead we chose quartzite. Quartzite is stain resistant if messes are wiped up promptly. I am a neat freak, so this countertop option is perfect for me and my family. Another benefit of quartzite is that it can give a marble vibe with that pretty, veiny quality of marble.

Keep in mind that some items are necessary to splurge on, such as new appliances, lighting, backsplash, and, of course, a good contractor. Spending more on these areas of the project will help you save money in the long run.

If your budget doesn't allow spending a bunch of money on your cabinets and countertops, there are five ways you can save and still come out with a great renovation. 1) Get your cabinets professionally spray-painted. 2) Shop at home good stores such as IKEA and The Home Depot for great cabinet options at a lower cost. 3) Consider different material options for your countertops. 4) Look for remnants, or leftover pieces cut for other projects, that you can buy from retailers at a bargain. 5) Buy locally and cut down on delivery costs.

No matter your needs, the best way to go about your kitchen project is to get several in-home estimates. A professional contractor can help you understand what costs what and how to allocate your funds. When you are working with a local contractor and/or designer, it's important to set and communicate a budget based on your needs. But be sure to add in money for unseen costs as well. As the old adage goes, "It's better to be safe than sorry!"

Pictured is my kitchen, which is where my family and I entertain guests, cook dinner, and play board games together. My husband, Jonathan, and I love drinking an occasional glass of wine and cooking a lot of Italian dishes. (Original New Jersey girl here, and boy, do I love spaghetti with marinara sauce!) Here you can see the quartzite countertop that best suits my family.

THE BUTLER'S PANTRY

What is a butler's pantry? Back in the day they were used to store a family's entertaining pieces, like formal serving trays, expensive china, and crystal. Most of the time these items were locked away to prevent theft from servants. These days, butler's pantries are used as additional food preparation space, storage space, coffee bars, or simple wine cellars. It is usually placed between the home's dining room and kitchen. If you enjoy entertaining, a butler's pantry can help with staging meals and supplying loads of counter space!

My butler's pantry is right off of the kitchen. I have to admit, the main reason I added it was because of the amazing additional storage it provides. (We have a tendency to hoard tea and coffee in my house.) It also serves as a great place to store my boys' after-school snacks. I put some of their applesauce packets in cute baskets that slide in and out of the cabinet. There's also a minifridge for adult beverages and sodas. It's the perfect little space.

Whether you need additional counter space for food preparation or extra storage like my family, you might want to look into adding a butler's pantry to your kitchen. I promise you, if you have the space and budget, they're amazing!

Gathering Table

THE DINING ROOM

A DINING ROOM IS A SPACE TO RECONNECT WITH MY FAMILY.

When I was growing up in the late '90s and early 2000s, my family dining room was used as a catchall of sorts. It was a room that we simply walked by while tossing on the table random papers, cookbooks, etc. We used it maybe twice a year for Christmas and Easter. Otherwise, the dining room was always an afterthought space.

I remember my mother reminiscing about her childhood one evening. She recalled her mother (my Nana) preparing meals for the family with care. Nearly every night they ate in their formal dining room together and discussed their daily activities.

When I became an interior designer, many clients asked me to repurpose their dining room. Clients wanted to turn them into home offices, game rooms, craft rooms, or homeschooling spaces. I happily completed these projects and made them into functional rooms for the family. However, deep down inside, I wondered about the allure of the formal dining room. Specifically, would it be chic to bring it back to my own home? I began to think that a dining room could be a space to revisit and reconnect with my family.

In the past years, it seemed other families began to feel the same as I did about dining rooms. During and after the Covid pandemic, dining rooms officially made a comeback for many people. Families were always busy running kids around to school events, sports games, and birthday parties, but during the pandemic, many people were forced to slow down and value the simple events of life. One of those events included eating a meal, which I have seen in the increase of clients requesting formal dining spaces. Now, more and more people are tired of eating in the kitchen or in front of the TV in family rooms. Instead, they are rediscovering that dining rooms are a perfect place to disconnect from technology and simply enjoy one another.

Pictured is the dining room of the historic house that we photographed for this book. It is beautifully extravagant, with nature-themed wallpaper, a great chandelier, and both a fireplace and mantle. There are also two entrances with a short set of stairs for each, making for a slightly grand entrance. The design is moody and eye-catching, and there is truly nothing boring about this formal dining room.

ADD A BIT OF DRAMA OR A STATEMENT PIECE.

PRO TIP

To make a dining space more elevated, add a bit of drama or a statement piece. A fireplace or mantle are great options. You can also save money by buying a mantle secondhand and painting it.

Not every dining room is the same. Some dining rooms are casual rooms off to the side while some are grand spaces with various entrances and exits. The common types of dining rooms include the formal dining room which is an individual room of its own. The pass-through dining room has open doorways that allow you to pass through it to get to another space of the home. And the informal or dual-purpose dining room may share space with a living room or kitchen. These are often seen in homes with open floor plans. (See page 178 in the Style Guide.)

Above is an example of a formal dining room. Opposite is a dual-purpose dining room that is in its own nook but open on one side so that it flows into the kitchen.

CHOOSING THE RIGHT TABLE SHAPE DEPENDS ON THE SIZE AND SHAPE OF YOUR DINING ROOM.

No matter the type of dining room you want to have in your home, the table size and shape are important when making it functional.

Choosing the right table shape depends on the size and shape of the room. Start by measuring: measure each wall, the distance between the walls, and the height of the ceiling. Also measure the distances between the trim, chair rail, and molding if you have them.

Next, decide on the shape of the table. If you have a smaller dining room, shaped like a square, I suggest a circular table. This will create more space to walk around. If your dining room is a thin rectangle shape, then I would suggest a rectangular or oval table.

Finally, remember that dining rooms often have hutches and cabinets. If you want them, plan space for these extra items around your dining table. In the photo opposite, the dining room is opened to the kitchen, so there's extra counter space and lots of cabinetry. The gorgeous antique wooden table with the original benches also adds a traditional element. Paired with modern chairs and décor allows it to fit seamlessly with the rest of the space, while also being a focal piece.

DINING ROOM WALLS

Once you have the main pieces of furniture picked out, it's time to turn your attention to the walls. Dining rooms do not have to be stuffy and boring, but colorful paint is not the only thing that can bring vibrance to a space. As a formal dinner space, for a touch of design intrigue, I always recommend going bold with wallpaper. My favorite options are fun botanical prints and textured grass cloth.

If you don't want to paint or wallpaper, to keep your dining room from looking like a big white box, add some art and photos. In my projects, I often mix vintage- and modern-style prints for an overall interesting yet stylish vibe. You can even add a gallery wall! The best thing about a gallery wall is that it's a classical design option and will never go out of style. (Pictured is an example of a dining room with a gallery wall.)

While costly, you can also add a fireplace for glamor and sophistication. If you do not have the budget to add a fireplace, go for a vintage mantel to create a faux fireplace. I did this in my old home, and it looked very cool.

The last piece of décor I want to mention are built-in bars. If you have the space for it, a built-in bar can be added along a blank wall. Not only will this be functional, but it also adds style. After all, we need to make sure that the ingredients for our cocktails are within reach! To get around spending a bunch of money to install a built-in bar, you can also add a console table or cabinet. These are smaller options, but you'll still be able to display your best dishes or have an area to create a grazing table or dessert bar within the dining room.

Dream Oasis

THE PRIMARY BEDROOM

THE PRIMARY BEDROOM IS THE MOST PERSONAL SPACE IN THE HOME.

The first thing that comes to mind when I think about my bedroom is getting into bed at the end of the day and turning on true crime. (Yes, I love my true crime shows. Guilty!) The idea makes me so happy; nothing can beat it!

The primary bedroom is, in my opinion, the most personal space in the home. Many of my clients want their bedroom to feel like a luxurious hotel where the stress of the day vanishes. Your primary bedroom should be a place where you can wind down, relax, and feel the utmost comfort. It should also have a sense of calm that is complemented by your design style. So, let's start at the top: the paint.

My clients will often ask me what color they should paint their bedroom. My answer is always the same: choose whatever color makes *you* the happiest. However, there are some things you should know.

Bright colors, such as yellows, reds, and oranges, tend to increase your heart rate and therefore might make you feel more awake. They are the *worst* colors for sleep. The *best* colors that make you feel calm are often mellow tones, such as creamy whites, soothing blues, and earthy greens. My favorite blue paint color of all time is Benjamin Moore Boothbay Grey. (I used it for the bedroom in my old home, as you can see in the photo.) However, as much as I loved having a blue bedroom, when we moved to our current home, I wanted to give an all-white bedroom a try. We ended up choosing Benjamin Moore White Dove. (For more, see page 188 in the Style Guide).

Before we get into the ways you can make your bedroom stylish and functional, the bedroom layout is an important factor because we want to make the most of our space no matter the size. When you think of the bedroom, usually, the bed is flanked by two nightstands. Across from the bed is a TV or dresser. That's really all you need, right? Typically, yes, but, every home and bedroom, whether they are old or new, have their own dimensions and room quirks.

The most standard primary bedroom layout that looks the best includes the bed placed at the center of the longest wall with no windows. Beds placed in front of the windows will block the light. If you have two windows that are separated on the same wall, place the bed in between them. See the photo below of my primary bedroom where I currently have this setup.

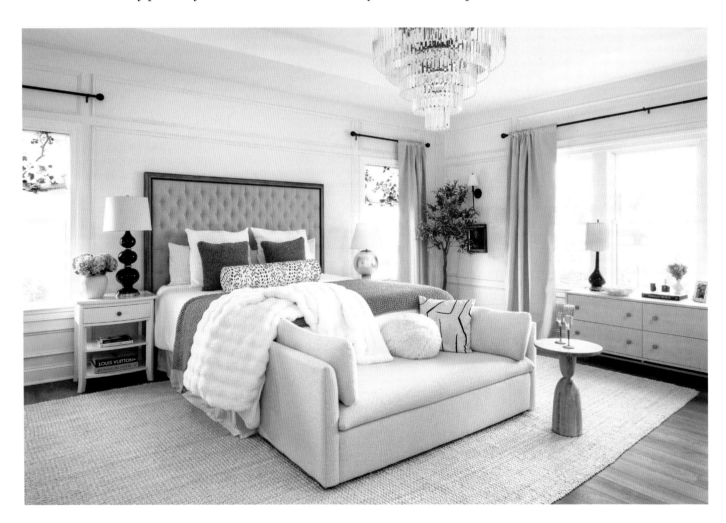

With larger bedrooms, it's important to divide the room into areas. We want the room to appear spacious and airy but not random and lonely. Also remember that the scale of furniture is crucial. (After finishing this section, make sure to read Scale and Proportion in the Style Guide on page 138 for more explanation on this.) You want to add larger pieces to a room of a larger size. If the furniture is tiny in scale to the room, it gives the space a cluttered feel.

In the front area of my bedroom, I have a mantle with a fireplace and a small conversation area that separates the sleeping area. A small couch sits at the end of the bed with a table and a bench for extra seating. Then, on the right side of the room is a small writing desk that I use as a multipurpose vanity—I keep my jewelry here and it's a quiet place to sit and read.

The other areas in my bedroom include a chair with a small gallery wall above it in the corner, just behind the door (see the photo opposite). On the same wall, but in the other corner, we created a small nook with an accent chair and some task lighting (see the photo below and page 41). It's a great little reading corner and adds more seating and purpose to the large space. (For more, see page 180 in the Style Guide.)

CURTAINS

Curtains in the bedroom play a huge role! (The same rules for the bedroom can also be applied to the living room.) First, hang your curtain rod high up near the ceiling instead of on the windowsill. The goal is for your curtains to extend to the floor, give or take an inch. Long curtains are not only pretty but they visually elongate the room. Curtains with vertical thin stripes will also give the illusion of higher ceilings.

There are various styles of curtains you can choose from. They can completely block any outside light, such as blackout curtains, or they can allow a certain level of light to shine through, such as room-darkening, light-filtering, and sheer curtains. I suggest adding dual window treatments. In other words, having sheer curtains behind blackout curtains will look luxurious and keep out the morning rays (the photo shows a good example of this).

Another option is to add drapes or a Roman shade underneath the curtains. If you choose to add Roman shades to your window treatments, know these bits of information: Roman shades come in a variety of natural weaves and fabrics that you can choose from. There are also two ways of hanging a Roman shade. They can be hung as an inside mount or an outside mount. Outside mount shades are mounted on the outside of the window frames directly onto the wall or ceiling. Inside mounts are placed inside the window frame. I have mine as an inside mount.

Having Roman shades that open upward and curtains that open sideways helps you better control the light and privacy of a room. You can find Roman shades in styles of pleated, flat, relaxed, and cascade. (In the photo, you can see that I have both Roman shades and curtains in my primary bedroom.) Not only is layering windows aesthetically pleasing, but it also provides high insulation—closer to the window, they help combat summer heat at its entry point and have extra fabric that keeps the cold out in the winter.

Now that you have the layout of the room decided, it's time to discover what style is your personal favorite. Knowing your preferred style will help when selecting furniture and accessories and ensure that all the pieces work together. The best way to discover your personal design style is to source images of interiors or furniture that catch your eye. Pinterest and Instagram are a huge help for me!

Here are a few bedroom styles I know best: Glam style includes chrome fixtures, animal-print rugs, modern art, tufted beds, and mirrored nightstands. Traditional style includes historical brass chandeliers, vintage art, Persian rugs and nightstands, and warm wood bed frames with white linens. Modern style includes monochrome, bouclé and cane textures, brass hardware, and mid-century modern light fixtures. Eclectic style includes wavy velvet beds, funky art and pillows, jute rugs, modern chandeliers, and gourd table lamps. Farmhouse style includes overall lighter tones, cozy white bedding, natural wood table lamps, cotton rugs, black light fixtures, and traditional animal art.

Those are just a few examples of bedroom styles and the objects that are used in each. If any of these scream at you, dig deeper into it. I always suggest doing some research and compiling pieces that you love. When you take a step back, you should be able to see what style best suits your tastes.

My guest bedroom (pictured) is an example of a traditional-style bedroom with vintage art on the walls, a Persian rug, and warm wood with white linens.

In order for your room to feel stylish yet warm, adding a rug is crucial and can pull the look together instantly. Many of my clients ask what size rug they should use in their bedroom. They also ask where to place it. Most of that depends on the size of your bed and the size of your room. (Find measurements on page 162 in the Style Guide.)

If you do not want a rug that takes up too much space, or do not have the budget for it, at least make sure that your rug accommodates your bedside tables and bench at the end of your bed if you have one. Also make sure that upon getting out of the bed in the morning, the rug is beneath you. Nobody likes frozen feet!

One big mistake we see often as designers is small rug runners placed around the bed. People believe this is a better use of their money because most of the rug is not hidden under the bed. The issue with rug runners is that the rug has no anchor because the bed is not normally placed on top of it. The runner(s) then creates a cluttered and messy look from getting constantly moved and shoved around every time it's walked on. One solid large rug is a stunning visual in the bedroom.

LIGHTING IN THE BEDROOM IS CRUCIAL.

PRO TIP

For creating a relaxing mood, proper lighting in the bedroom is crucial. Use task lighting (page 41) to layer multiple forms of lighting to create that luxurious aesthetic.

Your nightstand lamp is an important task lighting (page 41), so I wanted to take a minute to talk more in depth about how to find the right one for your room. First, buy your nightstand . Most nightstands range from 24 to 28 inches (61 to 71 cm) tall. The best practice is to pick a nightstand that is 2 inches (5 cm) higher than your mattress. Then, buy the lamp. One rule when choosing the right lamp is to make sure the bottom of the shade is around chin level when you are sitting up in bed while reading or watching TV. Not only does this look aesthetically pleasing, but it also keeps the harsh light away from your eyes.

As a design rule of thumb, most people choose to have a nightstand light on each side of the bed as it's good for balance. However, for your bedroom choose as many lights as you want. (Also, nightstands *do not* have to match. For a cleaner look, pair together two nightstands of the same height and size. But for an asymmetrical look, use two that have different heights.)

Lastly, choose the correct size lampshade. Long before I began my interior design career, I purchased lampshades that were either much too big or way too small. I'll never forget all the times I had to repeatedly return lamps because I was simply guessing what size would work. As far as sizing goes, a table lamp should take up about one-third of the nightstand surface. The larger your primary room is, the larger the lamp should be, but the lampshade should never be larger or wider than the top of your nightstand. This can look overwhelming to the eye.

These photos are spaces in my guest bedroom. As a standard-sized bedroom, I was able
to fill the space around the bed with some chairs in a small conversation area as well as add
slightly larger décor.

Rejuvenation Zone

THE PRIMARY BATHROOM

Homeowners remodel their bathrooms for many reasons. Maybe you moved into a new home with an outdated bathroom. Maybe you want to add a tub. Or you want to change the tile to reflect your style. No matter the reason, updating your bathroom is a great way to increase your home's value!

According to *Remodeling Magazine*'s Cost vs. Value Report, a bathroom renovation adds about 55 to 65 percent of its price back into the home's value for resale. One thing I will say is that every bathroom project is not the same, mainly because every homeowner desires a different end goal.

Any type of bathroom remodel varies in pricing. A cosmetic refresh is the most cost-effective bathroom remodel. It helps update the overall aesthetic of the bathroom through surface-level changes. This can include a repainted vanity, fresh wall paint, new wallpaper, replaced hardware, new flooring, and plumbing fixtures.

An intermediate remodel goes a little deeper than cosmetics. Intermediate remodels, on top of surface-level changes, also include a possible new vanity and flooring. This one's a bit more invasive than a cosmetic refresh.

A complete remodel is also referred to as "gutting" the bathroom. This means you'll be starting from scratch—removing walls, redoing the plumbing system, and making changes to the overall floor plan. In other words, this will be the priciest update.

A FUNCTIONAL BATHROOM

Everyone wants their bathrooms not only to be functional but also beautiful to look at. Over the next few pages, I will give you five key tips to help you have a beautiful-looking and a fully functional bathroom.

Starting off, try and hide your toilet. For a spa-like vibe, find a reason to put the toilet in the background. While everyone needs a toilet in their bathroom, it's not the prettiest thing to look at! Try hiding the toilet with a low-angled wall or a small room that you can shut the door to if it is within your budget. Instead, and depending on your budget, make the focal point the beautiful tile flooring, a lighting fixture, or a chic tub.

You should also choose your vanity size wisely. If you buy a vanity that's too big, it can interfere with the walking space and create an impractical bathroom. If you pick a vanity that's too small, it can limit the much-needed countertop or storage space. The first step in making the right decision for your bathroom is measuring. In other words, make sure the vanity doors open easily without hitting any toilets and/or other doors.

PRO TIP

My number-one piece of advice when starting to design a room on your own is to create a focal point. This is a *great* place to start for any kind of bathroom renovation. As mentioned earlier, the focal point can be a large piece of art, a TV, a feature wall with painted wainscoting, big windows, or anything that commands attention. Once you have chosen your focal point, position your furniture around it. Make sure the furniture directs the eyes to the focal point. It should be easily visible.

CONVERTING YOUR TUB INTO A SHOWER IS AESTHETICALLY PLEASING AND COST EFFECTIVE.

This tip is geared toward shower people. I am one of those people who *only* takes showers; I rarely ever take baths. If you are like me and have a tub, consider converting your tub into a shower. By removing an unused tub, you gain 5 feet (1.5 m) of space to play with! And with a simple swap, you won't have to reroute plumbing. In other words, this update is aesthetically pleasing and cost effective.

In the tub or shower, always remember to make niches for your toiletries, especially if you are redoing the shower. Gone are the days of '90s plastic over-the-showerhead organizers. Instead, add a recessed cubby in the shower that can hold shampoos and conditioners.

Let's not forget the shower lighting (which is often overlooked)! In the shower area, choose a ceiling light that is rated for wet areas. They have features such as rubber gaskets or glass lenses that make the light moisture resistant. LED lights are often a great choice for the shower. They are also modern looking and energy efficient.

BATHROOM LIGHTING

One of the biggest tips I give my clients when it comes to bathrooms is to be mindful of the lighting scheme. Our bathrooms are usually the place where we apply makeup, brush our teeth, wash our face, and shave. In other words, lighting is important! We need it to see the smallest details, and no one likes leaning into a mirror for an extended period of time and maybe nearly breaking their backs.

The best rule of thumb is to try for around 50 lumens per square foot (4.6 lumens per m^2). The exact lumens you will need depend on the overall size of your bathroom. General lighting types to look for are ambient lighting that illuminates the whole space, task lighting (page 41) for illumination for specific tasks, and accent lighting as supplementary lighting to illuminate dark corners.

If you have a large bathroom, it's best, for both function and aesthetic, to choose a large chandelier or pendant for overhead lighting. If your bathroom is large but has low ceilings, do not worry! There are some incredible flush mount designs that will give you a stylish impact.

Pictured is a bathroom with lights above the mirror and a window at the right. In a modern style, the wallpaper and countertop are white with contrasting black accents sprinkled around that still allow for a bright space.

YOU CAN MAKE AN OLDER BATHROOM FEEL NEW AND UPDATED ON A BUDGET.

PRO TIP

There are so many ways you can make an older bathroom feel new and updated on a budget. Before we leave the bathroom, some final tips to help you save during a bathroom remodel include reselling old bathroom basins or brassware, painting instead of wallpapering, a simple reglazing of ugly tiles, and painting tile grout.

Imagination
Station

THE KIDS' ROOMS

INCLUDE THE CHILD IN THE DESIGN PROCESS AND ACKNOWLEDGE THEIR INDIVIDUAL INTERESTS.

In children's rooms, I let my whimsical side loose! I look for fun patterned wallpaper and soothing, yet chic, paint combinations. I have to admit that designing kids' rooms is among my favorite projects.

With that being said, it's important to include the child in the design process and acknowledge their individual interests. We want this to feel like their space and the only one who knows how to best create that space is the child themself. However, this is a potential roadblock for many parents, caretakers, and designers when it comes to designing kids' spaces. Here the bomb drops!

When it comes to designing my clients' kids' rooms, parents often request that their child is able to grow into the space. In other words, the room should not be overly childlike or babyish. Parents also request that the child's interests are included. So, how can we, as those designing the room, dedicate the room to the children while also mixing in adult sensibilities and a touch of sophistication? No one wants to spend a lot of money on items that are going to need to be replaced sooner rather than later. I recommend dedicating a wall to the child's hobbies. It adds that childlike feel and personality to the space that costs less and can be easily replaced. In the same vein of a gallery wall, hang your largest item in the center above a piece of furniture and have fun filling up the space!

DECORATING AND REVAMPING

While I love working with children when designing their dream bedroom, I only do so to a certain extent. The kiddos often request a saturation of their favorite cartoon or TV character. By saturation, I mean everything everywhere. For example, my youngest son is currently six years old and loves Baby Yoda (aka Grogu). When it came to designing his bedroom in our new house, he requested Baby Yoda bedding, art, lamps, wallpaper, toys, pillows, wall decals . . . you get the gist! He is pretty much obsessed.

While I am also a big fan of Baby Yoda (he is SO cute) the thought of an entire room dedicated to him made me dizzy. I knew my son's room should be a space where he feels safe and comfortable, and also reflects his interests. In the end, I made sure to add Baby Yoda touches without overkill. Which is to say, he already had lots of Baby Yoda plushies, sheets, books, and even a small table lamp. All of these things can be easily replaced when his Baby Yoda phase is over. With that in mind, I left all of these décor items on display and designed around it by matching colors and playing with texture and fabric. This decision meant that the room had elements of Baby Yoda in it without having to buy dedicated pieces of wallpaper or furniture, which would cost more money to replace. (See the photo for how it turned out.)

There are tons of storage options to choose from when thinking about organizational methods for a kids' room. Not only do children have a lot of stuff, but toys look cluttered when they are out and cannot be tucked away. From a simple wicker basket to something in a fun shape or design, the options are endless. If there is ever an opportunity to add in a playful piece of furniture that doesn't cost you too much to someday replace, buying fun storage is not a bad way to go about it. Some items you could purchase include patterned storage benches, colored dressers from places like Wayfair, a colorful hanging shoe rack, a corner book and toy organizer, or a whale-shaped wicker toy bin. You might, however, limit the number of whale-shaped baskets as you don't want to go overboard (pun intended).

Pictured is a kid's room I did for one of my clients. They had a blue-and-white nautical theme for their child. Because the room was quite small, the striped wallpaper was a great way to add some height and make the room look larger. The matching furniture and drawer handles added to the theme while also creating function in the space.

My older son, who is currently ten, tends to gravitate toward the color green. He is also an academic at heart. He loves to read and have sleepovers with his friends. For the design of his bedroom, he chose a dark academia green paint and asked for large bookshelves. We chose to place built-in bookshelves on the wall with the window and included a window seat that he could use for reading. We also purchased a day trundle bed in the same green color as his room. The trundle bed is a great choice as it saves a lot of space that can instead be used for play. It's also perfect for his sleepover parties because it includes a pull-out bed.

While every child is different, designing their rooms can be the most fun part of any home renovation. Enjoy it and create the spaces your children will love for a long time.

Thinking Space

THE HOME OFFICE

MOST PEOPLE NEED A SPACE FOR WORKING IN PEACE AND QUIET.

Since the Covid pandemic, with more people working from home, lots of my clients have asked for a revamp of their home office. By "revamp" I mean several things, such as transforming an existing, unused guest room into an office space, redoing a current home office, or creating an attic nook into a small office since every home does not always have an office space.

Regardless of your home office circumstances, most people need a space for working in peace and quiet. For the design process, I first ask clients what their needs are for the space. Some questions I typically ask include: Do you work from home full-time? Do you have clients come to your home office? Do you need a printer? Do you need bookshelves? How much storage do you need?

Every person has a different set of needs. Plus, we all work differently! As a result, there are no set rules on how to makeover your home office. My best advice is, if you don't already have a designated area to start with, choose a place that has as little distractions as possible. This could mean an out-of-the-way extra bedroom, a basement, or setting up a small desk in your bedroom in a quiet spot.

The next thing you'll want to figure out is what kind of mood you want your office to have. Your work area should provide a space where you can work at your best. There are a few common styles to choose from. Modern organic means light woods and metals, natural paint tones, and black-and-beige-colored accessories. Or you could go with modern glam with lots of gold finishes, animal prints, and a light blush paint. If you want to go all out, you can simply choose a moody style. This would include deeper-colored paint, dark woods, dramatic lighting, and rich textures.

ORGANIZING A HOME OFFICE

My current home office happens to be a room off my entryway. It's the first large office space I have ever had, which was something that was very important to me as my design business grew. As a designer, I needed a quiet room to work on client projects, make phone calls, send emails, and focus. I also knew I needed plenty of storage and a large desk.

For my desk, I chose the Reid Oval desk from CB2 because it's long and has ample storage. The curves are push-to-open doors with a frame. It makes for the perfect place to hide a large and bulky piece of technology, so I keep my printer here.

I added built-in bookshelves on the back wall for the tons of design books, art, candles, and other knickknacks I own. My husband is very handy, so we built and painted these shelves together as a DIY project when we moved in. The cabinets provide great storage to keep confidential paperwork organized.

For the best work from home experience, you also want to get the layout right. Every office has its limitations, but you should always 1) place your desk on the wall opposite the door, 2) add shelving or storage units against the wall, and 3) set up a conversation area with a sofa or chairs if you have the room. In my case, I didn't have room for a conversation area, but I did add a mantle that currently serves as decoration and more storage for my books. (For more, see page 184 in the Style Guide.)

Lighting should be prioritized in home offices because good lighting can increase your productivity and overall mood. (For more, see page 169 in the Style Guide.)

In general, warmer yellow lights tend to work well for in-home offices when creating a relaxing feel. Another tip is to avoid the harsh glare of overhead lights. Instead, search for wall sconces or desk lamps that do not overpower the space. In other words, create task lighting (page 41).

When I'm working at my desk or reading client paperwork, I use an adjustable arm table lamp to help me see what I am doing. I also added wall sconces to the back wall so I can easily clean or file paperwork in my cabinets.

Finally, don't forget to utilize natural light whenever you can. Sunlight is beneficial for the mood and can improve the overall work environment. Just make sure any natural light faces the back of your computer to avoid that annoying glare. Since sunlight can be overpowering some days, I also suggest investing in window treatments. You can try simple blinds or stylish darkening drapes.

PART TWO

STYLE GUIDE

TIME FOR ALL THE NITTY-GRITTY DETAILS.

Now that we have discussed the most significant rooms in your home, it's time to get down to business. In other words, the specifics when it comes to measuring, fabrics, colors, and all the little elements that make a design come together. Comfortable interior design in your home should evoke happiness and soothe the stresses of the day. Coming back to a beautiful and cozy home does wonders for the soul. We all want thoughtfully designed rooms that will enhance the quality of our day-to-day life. Whether this means promoting relaxation in spaces we wish to wind down, or creating energy where energy is needed, in this section I will walk you through creating functional layouts and aesthetically pleasing designs.

DESIGN BASICS

Many of us were not born with the skills to arrange rooms, knock out walls, design kitchens, select art, choose paint colors, and select the right contractors for our home's interior design. Only if we choose to study it do we learn all these things over time. Whether you are a design student or just want to style your home, I am here to give you all the tips and tricks you need to know to get started with confidence.

Before we begin, you should first know the difference between an "interior designer" and an "interior decorator." People commonly mistake them as being the same job; however, they are not.

An interior designer is someone who makes indoor spaces functional, safe, and stylish. Many designers work with architects and can read and edit blueprints of homes and corporate spaces. An interior decorator simply focuses on the aesthetic décor of the room. For example, a decorator does not make the call to knock down walls and change the layout of the home.

When thinking about interior design, you want to know exactly what you're looking for and what you need. The following sections will go over some design basics that are my go-tos when it comes to designing a client's, or my own, space.

THE SEVEN PRINCIPLES OF DESIGN

Design is a skill that can be learned and honed into an ability that comes naturally. To begin crafting a beautiful living space, these seven concepts will guide you and provide comprehension. They will allow you to figure out what a space needs, what it lacks, and how to make it better.

1. BALANCE

A harmonious balance of the room's components can visually stabilize a space. In other words, balance ensures that nothing in the room overtakes another. We want everything to fit and work together.

2. UNITY

Unity refers to similar items and repetition in the room's details, such as patterns. The goal is to help pull everything together and make it cohesive throughout. Unity can be seen in one room of the home or across multiple rooms.

3. SCALE

Scale refers to how furniture fits in a given room. The right scale is determined by the size of a space. For example, a room with high ceilings would benefit from taller furniture instead of smaller pieces.

4. COLOR

A balanced room scheme needs to have proper proportional colors, or understanding how colors interact with each other. We will go more in depth on this topic when discussing the Design Rules on page 142. For now, choose a color story and decide how you want to apply those colors throughout the space (i.e., in pieces of furniture, fabrics, hardware, etc.).

5. TEXTURE

Texture is the surface of a material that can be experienced through touch. When designers say they are "adding texture" to a room this means they are incorporating materials with various finishes and smoothness levels to achieve a space that feels cozy and stylish. Different textures also add visual importance and make an object stand out.

6. PATTERN

Mixing patterns is a common thing an interior designer does to give a room dimension. The patterns do not have to match; however, they must complement one another. Designers do this by thinking of scale, size, and color. (For more on this, see Mixing Patterns on page 152.)

7. EMPHASIS

Rooms need a focal point that draws attention as soon as you walk in. Emphasis can be many things such as a large sofa, a colorful piece of art, a marble fireplace, or dramatic windows. (I recommend purchasing these items from high-end shops, as I describe on page 192.)

THEME AND FLOW

How do you choose a style for the entire house? Interior design is a very personal thing. You want your home to feel like yours and represent your family. But while all the little decorations and finishing touches can be unique to the room, having a flow throughout the entire house is the key to creating a great interior design.

COLOR SCHEME

Pick your go-to color and place it in every room, whether in large focal-point items, or small décor pieces. Then create a color story centered around your main color. (See page 188.)

FLOORING

Flooring will be in every room of the house, and it's not cheap. Choose flooring based on your color story and make sure it suits you and your lifestyle. (See page 144.)

HARDWARE

Having only one metal throughout the entire house can make it seem one-dimensional. Choose a few (one to three) that matches both your color story and flooring. (See page 164.)

WALLPAPER

Some people love wallpaper; others don't like it much. I *love* wallpaper. Decide whether or not you will be adding wallpaper and in which rooms. They are great for adding vibrance and texture to a space. But make sure to use the correct type when installing it in high-moisture rooms. (I give more detail about this on page 210.)

CABINETRY

There are so many styles of cabinets you can use for your kitchen—and carry on in other rooms in storage and organizational units. Go back to your personal style and flooring to decide on a style and color.

COUNTERTOPS

Countertops can be a huge money drinker, but thankfully there are plenty to choose from, including hacks where you can get the finish you want without spending too much. I recommend looking into slab granite, marble, and quartzite. If you go for a natural stone, a rule of thumb is to never let a substance "soak in" for too long. This is because natural stones can be porous and prone to drag liquids into the material.

LIGHTING

From chandeliers to pendants to sconces and so many more, lighting occurs in every room. We've already touched on lighting fixtures in a given room throughout the book, but you should also think about the fixtures you want in your home when it comes to amount, style, and hardware. (For more, see page 166.)

SCALE AND PROPORTION

Scale dictates the overall feel of a room. It is the understanding of how the size of one object relates to the size of the room. For example, a king-size bed in a small bedroom is the wrong scale. Proportion is understanding the scale of a single object in comparison to the other objects in a room. This includes size, shape, texture, and color.

FURNITURE TO ROOM SIZE

Let's start with the living room. Most often, the sofa is the main piece of furniture. If you have an overstuffed sofa in a small family room a designer would say that the sofa is off scale for this room. Instead, for large rooms use bigger main pieces of furniture and vice versa for small rooms.

FURNITURE TO CEILINGS

If you live in a home with high ceilings, look for large and tall furniture. Small chairs will look off in a room with high ceilings. It is better to purchase one or a couple of tall or large pieces of furniture instead of multiple small pieces as too many small pieces can look sloppy. On the other hand, lower ceilings need low furniture and décor. One exception to this rule is the style that intentionally uses low modern furniture in rooms with high ceilings. In this case, add trim such as dentil molding to the top of the room to maximize the space and draw the eye up.

PATTERNS TO ROOM SIZE

If you have a large room, large patterns will look dramatic and chic. The room can also handle more color. If you are decorating a small room, keep the patterns on a smaller scale so that they repeat a few times. This will help with the room's balance.

NEGATIVE SPACE

We do not want a room to look overly busy and cluttered with furniture and collectables. Negative space not only leaves space for walking but also allows general breathing room. In other words, the décor doesn't overwhelm the room. When thinking about a room's proportion, make sure there is enough negative space once it's fully designed.

FOCAL POINT

In a bedroom, the bed is usually the focal point fixed in a central point of the room. After choosing a bed to your liking, build the rest of your design around your bed. In the dining room, build around the dining table. This rule applies no matter the size of the room.

REPEAT PATTERNS

It is pleasing to the eye to see patterns and colors reused throughout the home. For example, if you have rectangle windows, try a rectangle coffee table, rug, décor, etc. The same goes for actual patterns, fabrics, and colors.

TAKING MEASUREMENTS

1. SKETCH

The first thing you want to do is roughly sketch the room, noting where the windows, doors, and fixed furniture pieces are located. This does not need to be pretty or to scale.

2. MEASURE

Next, get your tape measure. The longer the tape measure, the better. Ideally, 25 feet (8 m) is the minimum length yours should be so that you can measure the entire room easily.

3. LENGTH AND WIDTH

The first thing you'll want to measure is the general length and width of the room. Do this by measuring the walls. Then measure the doors, windows, and any other larger built-in pieces. These dimensions should also include their distance from the floor and ceiling.

4. FIXED OBJECTS

Lastly, measure and note the locations of, and the distance between, outlets, light switches, thermostats, air vents/returns, baseboards, crown molding, light fixtures, and so on.

DESIGN RULES

There are six design rules you should know when you're designing a space. I will cover them all here so that you can begin making smart design decisions and make your place feel like home.

60:30:10 RULE

60% Dominant Color	30% Supporting Color	10% Accent Color
Walls	Furniture	Accessories
Large Furniture	Accent Walls	Throw Pillows
Rug	Cabinets	Candles
Fabric	Bookshelves	Picture Frames
	Small Tables	Curtains

Use this design rule when you're thinking about what colors to add to a room. This rule allows you to use the colors you want to use in an organized, but not overwhelming, manner. The formula is 60 percent of the room should be a dominant color (walls, large furniture pieces, rugs, fabrics), 30 percent should be a secondary color (accent furniture, accent walls, cabinets, bookshelves, small tables), and 10 percent should be the remainder (accessories, throw pillows, candles, picture frames, curtains). This may sound confusing, so I've included the following visual example.

70:30 RULE

As a designer, I love to mix décor styles for an effortless yet cohesive look. This is called "juxtaposition." To follow this design rule, divide your room into a ratio of 70:30. This means that you will design 70 percent of the space with your main scheme and 30 percent in a different but complementary style. For example, I love to design a room with 70 percent traditional décor and mix in 30 percent modern décor. In the living room I will have a traditional sofa, traditional rug, traditional lighting, and classical wall paint, with a modern piece of art and modern throw pillows.

2:3 RULE

This rule relates to furniture, specifically the ratio of the largest (or focal) piece of furniture in a room. Think about your living room. The sofa is usually the largest piece in the space. To select the correct size sofa, it should take up a ratio of 2:3 of the room's area.

THE GOLDEN RATIO, OR 60:40 RULE

This rule helps designers achieve visual balance when adding all the furniture into a room. This rule works for any room in your house. You should fill 60 percent of your floor space with furniture and leave 40 percent open. By following this rule, the room won't feel overcrowded or empty.

TRIANGLE OF LIGHTING RULE

All rooms must have decent lighting to create warmth and ambiance. If you are using lamps to light a room, it's important that they create a "triangle." This is strictly so the room has ample lighting, and things feel balanced. Having only one source of light in the room can make it feel flat.

RULE OF THREE

Did you know that our eyes are naturally drawn to groups of three? Our brains just love odd numbers, and groupings of three tend to look natural to the human eye. The best and easiest way to follow the rule of three is to purchase three different sizes of the same object and place them in the room together. Or combine two smaller pieces with one large piece.

FLOORING

Flooring is another item that will be in every room of your home. This can be an intimidating choice since there are many types of flooring to choose from, as well as selecting the right tones like cool, neutral, and warm. Flooring is not cheap, so let's break down the different types that you may be considering. Whether you are replacing old flooring in your current home or building a home from scratch, it's important to make sure you choose what is best for you and your lifestyle.

HARDWOOD

ENGINEERED WOOD OR MAN-MADE WOOD

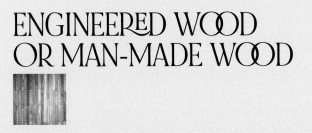

BAMBOO

PARQUET

CORK

PROS

This type of flooring has been popular in homes all over the world. It is milled from timber, beautiful to look at, water resistant, easy to clean, and very durable. Walnut, oak, pine, and hickory are common types of wood flooring.

Great for homeowners who love the wood look without it being real wood. It is made up of layers, with a genuine wood veneer layer on top. It's more resilient than hardwood flooring when dealing with moisture and it's easy to install.

Slightly harder than most hardwood options, it is extremely strong and durable with a natural sandy blond color. It is also environmentally friendly.

Parquet was originally created to replace marble in sixteenth-century France because it is much lighter to transport and carry. Parquet is hardwood flooring that is joined together (usually glued down) to make a pattern. It is very durable, allergy friendly, and sustainable.

An eco-friendly and durable option. It is bark harvested from cork oak trees and soft underfoot.

CONS

Hardwood is higher in price than other types of flooring on the market. It also does not retain heat.

Be careful who you purchase engineered wood from because quality can differ from brand to brand.

Bamboo is susceptible to water damage and, over time, can fade in heavily sunlit areas.

Parquet tends to warp if used in damp rooms, such as bathrooms and basements. Also, if you plan on selling your home any time soon, avoid certain parquet patterns as some homebuyers may feel parquet is a dated look.

Cork can fade in the sunlight and is easily damaged by kids and pets. It also needs to be resealed every five to seven years.

VINYL

STONE

CERAMIC/PORCELAIN

CARPET

PROS

CONS

A cost-friendly option, vinyl is a synthetic polymer flooring with added pigmentation for color. It is water resistant, flexible, and non-porous. It also comes in a variety of colors and designs.

Sharp edges of furniture can tear vinyl due to its softness.

This flooring's appearance improves over time, giving the home a traditional and classical aesthetic.

Stone is a more costly option, and it can be slippery when wet.

Easy to clean in indoor and outdoor spaces. Small imperfections will also be hard to detect, making it very durable.

Ceramic/porcelain is very hard underfoot, making it not the most comfortable choice.

Incredibly cozy underfoot, it dampens footsteps in the home and can act as a heat retainer in the cooler months. Installation varies depending on the type of carpet you choose.

Carpet easily stains in comparison to other types of flooring. Also, if placed in high-traffic areas, carpets can appear worn out.

FABRICS

Choosing the right fabrics for your lifestyle is helpful to know before you begin the buying process. You want your sofa and chairs to be comfortable as well as durable. If you have babies, children, and/or pets this is especially important. Luckily, nowadays, there are many options for not only stylish but stain-resistant fabric. The following list are the types of fabrics I recommend.

CRYPTON

I recommend crypton to my clients with large families and pets. Crypton comes in a variety of pretty styles and is stain, odor, and moisture resistant, and very easy to clean. The best part is that it's free of harsh chemicals.

WOOL OR WOOL BLEND

If you are not sold on crypton for your living room furniture, try wool or wool blends. This fabric is warm and durable and a great choice for kid-friendly homes because they do not wrinkle easily. You can also easily spot clean a wool chair or sofa.

SUEDE

The addition of suede to any living space will instantly add glamor. The problem is that it needs a lot of maintenance. Suede is not ideal for pets or kids, but it's great if you want a more stylish look.

VELVET

Velvet is my favorite fabric for chairs and sofas! Not only does it give a luxurious feel, but it's also relatively easy to maintain.

LEATHER

This fabric is a great material for avoiding stains because it can be easily wiped clean. The issue is that it can be easily scratched. As a result, I rarely recommend it to pet owners.

LINEN

This fabric is a popular choice for sofas and chairs. Linen is eco-friendly and hypoallergenic, making it a great natural fabric. After cleaning, it gets softer. Overall, it's not a bad choice.

POLYESTER

Polyester is very durable. It's made with synthetic fibers, which makes it less likely to break down over long periods of time. As a result, polyester is a good choice for households with pets and/or children. This material is also fade resistant!

NYLON

This fabric is often considered the best material for living room furniture. Nylon is inexpensive, durable, lightweight, and it dries quickly.

ACRYLIC

Acrylic is a nice alternative to wool as it's often claimed to be imitation wool. It's also UV resistant, which means it will not fade when left by a sunny window. These days acrylic comes in tons of colors and patterns.

FURNITURE STYLES

From sofas and chairs to dressers and drawers to knobs and hardware—let's quickly go through these items so that you're prepared to buy the right ones for every room.

TIGHT BACK

Tight back sofas are generally less deep than cushion back sofas because they do not have to accommodate cushions on their back. The positive about them is the back support as they hold a person in a more upright position. The negative is that many folks find it less comfortable when they want to lounge, such as in a family room. Tight backs can be anywhere on average from 34 to 38 inches (86 to 97 cm) deep. I recommend putting them in small rooms and home offices because they are firm and often look sophisticated.

CUSHION BACK

Cushion back sofas are deep sofas. They have both the back support as well as cushions. In general, they run about 36 to 42 inches (91 to 107 cm) deep. I recommend putting them in rooms where comfort is a priority, such as family rooms. I love sitting and watching a movie in a cozy cushion back sofa.

LOVE SEAT

These sofas generally seat two people. The average love seat length is around 58 to 66 inches (147 to 168 cm). Their average depth is 34 to 38 inches (86 to 97 cm). For types of love seats, refer back to tight back and cushion back above. You should purchase a love seat when you need extra seating or for smaller conversation areas.

APARTMENT-SIZE SOFA

A sofa with a length between love seats and regular sofas. Apartment-size sofas are about 20 to 30 inches (51 to 76 cm) shorter than the length of a full-size sofa. They may also be shallower in depth. These work well in small spaces when you still want to accommodate seating for other people

ACCENT CHAIRS

Accent chairs usually fit one person and have an elevated design that makes them stand out in a room. These chairs can range from wingback, club, bergère, barrel, mid-century modern, slipper, Lawson, English rolled arm, and fanback.

SOFA ARM TYPES

There are ten main types of sofa arm types, including track, modern scroll, track with nails, modern English, pleated, ruched, pad, key, shelter, and saddle.

WOODEN CHAIR BACKS

Wooden chair backs come in eclectic and intricate designs including, but not limited to, bentwood, sheaf, pierced splat, lath, banister, stick, bow, lyre, and square.

FURNITURE LEG STYLES

Styles for chairs, tables, and standing mirrors include double scroll, reversed scroll, walnut period, turned twist, cabriole, straight, Adam style, fluted, Sheraton tapered, Marlborough, saber, spade, and reeded.

MIXING PATTERNS

If you love adding patterns to your space, there are a few rules I live by. Especially when it comes to mixing multiple patterns together, we don't want it to look like a chaotic mess. This section will teach you all you need to know when it comes to mixing patterns that make a cohesive design.

PIT LARGE SCALE AGAINST SMALL SCALE

Find your focal pattern; this is usually a large-scale print that draws the eye whenever someone enters the room. Then, find other patterns to mix with it, usually small-scale patterns. In the photo example below, my guest bedroom has one accent wall with a small-striped wallpaper while the other walls are a solid color.

THREE PATTERNS

If you are using three patterns, choose patterns that are different in size and design but similar in color. As you can see in my guest bedroom in the photo below, the chairs have a large floral pattern, the rug is a medium Persian design, and the accent wall (see the bottom-left photo) has small white-and-blue-striped wallpaper.

FIVE PATTERNS

If you are using five patterns, I recommend going with one strong solid color, a large-scaled pattern, a medium-sized pattern, and two smaller patterns. For example, in my younger son's room, the strong solid color is in the carpet. The large-scaled pattern is in the checkerboard bed frame. The medium-sized pattern is the wallpaper. And the two small patterns are in the throw pillow and sconce light shade.

RUG TYPES

Rugs are so important when it comes to bringing together the design of a room. They add texture and color and soften the space. That said, there are so many styles and colors on the market these days that picking the one that best fits your space and style can be overwhelming. In this section, let's go over the common rug types you might be choosing from.

WOOL

This rug comes at a high cost but is well made. Wool rugs are often passed down from generation to generation because of their high quality. Personally, I love using wool rugs because they are easy to clean, they hold color perfectly, and are oh so soft. Wool is my first choice for rugs.

SILK

Silk rugs are shiny beauties and soft on the feet. The downfall is that they are difficult to clean because they are very delicate.

COTTON

Cotton rugs are great for casual spaces. They are budget friendly and a good alternative to wool rugs. The downfall is that they will not last for decades and will fade more quickly than other materials.

JUTE

Jute rugs are beautiful looking. They are also perfect for laying underneath smaller decorative rugs like faux animal hide rugs. However, jute tends to slide around easily on hardwood floors. You can still use them by placing furniture on top or using rug gripper tape. Jute rugs are also known to shed little fibers.

POLYPROPYLENE

These synthetic blend rugs are thinner than wool, making them budget friendly. They are also soft under the feet. They work well in high-traffic areas because they are easy to clean and fade resistant. They are also environmentally friendly; however, they do not decompose well.

WASHABLE

These days washable rugs come in a variety of styles and colors. Washable rugs are stain resistant, lightweight, and low maintenance. The downfall is that they can develop creases if folded for too long. Also, the rug designs are printed onto the rugs and not woven like a traditional rug. If you don't like the printed look, avoid these.

RUG SIZING

Rug sizes are also important! Selecting the wrong size rug can make your room look unbalanced. However, choosing a rug size can feel confusing at times. (Trust me, I get it!) Use the following sections to discover the best size and placement of a rug in every space.

RECOMMENDED AREA RUG SIZE TO ROOM SIZE

ROOM SIZE	RUG SIZE
5 x 7 ft (1.5 x 2 m)	3 x 5 ft (1 x 1.5 m)
7 x 10 ft (2 x 3 m)	5 x 8 ft (1.5 x 2.4 m)
10 x 12 ft (3 x 4 m)	8 x 10 ft (2.4 x 3 m)
11 x 14 ft (3.4 x 4 m)	9 x 12 ft (3 x 4 m)
14 x 17 ft (4 x 5 m)	12 x 15 ft (4 x 5 m)

SOFAS AND SECTIONALS

The most common sizes for living room rugs are 8 x 10 feet (2 x 3 m) and
9 x 12 feet (3 x 4 m). For larger rooms, 10 x 14 feet (3 x 4 m) can be used as well.
If the rug in the living space is too small, this can make the overall room appear
smaller than it is. The general rule of thumb is that an area rug should fit under
all the main furniture pieces. However, if you want a smaller rug, see the
example of the 8 x 5 feet (2 x 1.5 m) in the sofa diagram.

PLACEMENT

My recommendation is to place rugs 6 inches (15 cm) from the wall so that the room doesn't look cramped. You do not want the area rug to be too large and cover vents or bunch up against the walls. If you have a larger room, double the length.

ORIENTATION

Make sure the rug you choose is at least 6 to 7 inches (15 to 18 cm) wider than the sofa on both sides. This creates a balanced look. If you have a sectional sofa, the same rules apply. You can either place the sofa and chairs on the rug or around it.

SOFA

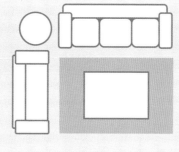

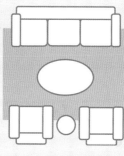

8 x 5 feet (2 x 1.5 m)   8 x 10 (2 x 3 m)

SECTIONAL

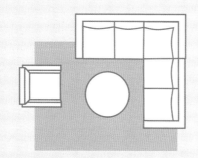
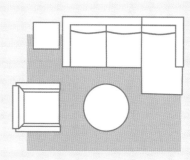

8 x 10 (2 x 3 m)   8 x 10 (2 x 3 m)

DINING TABLES

Let me start by saying that I love adding rugs in dining rooms. They add beauty, warmth, and texture. They can also dampen sound better than hardwood floors. You want to make sure the rug has the right weave. Dining room rugs should be flatweave made from durable synthetics like polypropylene or jute. Your family and guests will be moving about, and chairs will slide in and out. Flatweave rugs help chairs to slide easier.

PLACEMENT

Center the rug within the room. The general rule is to base the size of the rug on the size of your dining table. Take the size of your table and then add 24 to 30 inches (61 to 76 cm) to the height and length to get the correct size of your rug.

ORIENTATION

Position the rug under the table with enough room to move the chairs. You have the correct size when the dining chairs still remain on the rug when pulled out.

RECTANGULAR

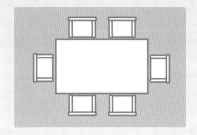 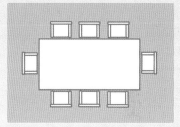

CIRCULAR

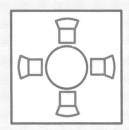 

BEDS

If you don't have carpeting in your bedroom, you'll most likely want to add a rug so that your feet don't touch the cold floor once you step out of bed. Even if you have carpeting, rugs can add another layer of design.

PLACEMENT

Make sure you leave 2 to 3 inches (5 to 8 cm) of the floor showing between the edge of the rug and the dresser. (You can leave up to 23 inches (58 cm) of space between the rug and dresser.)

ORIENTATION

The most common place for an area rug is under the bed. But make sure the rug doesn't push up against your dresser as that tends to look sloppy. If you want a large rug, make sure it slides neatly underneath the dresser.

TWIN

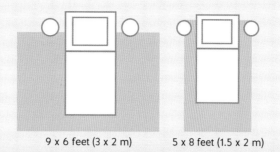

9 x 6 feet (3 x 2 m)   5 x 8 feet (1.5 x 2 m)

FULL

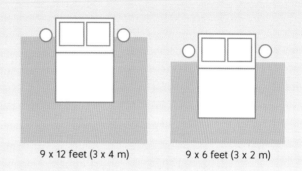

9 x 12 feet (3 x 4 m)   9 x 6 feet (3 x 2 m)

QUEEN

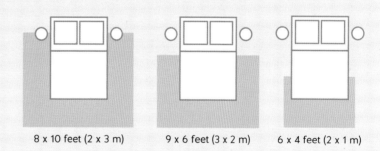

8 x 10 feet (2 x 3 m)   9 x 6 feet (3 x 2 m)   6 x 4 feet (2 x 1 m)

KING

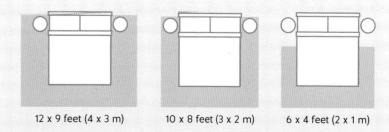

12 x 9 feet (4 x 3 m)   10 x 8 feet (3 x 2 m)   6 x 4 feet (2 x 1 m)

MIXING METALS

Let me start off by saying this: it is perfectly okay to mix metals in every room. As a matter of fact, I encourage it as it gives the room depth and interest. Here are my tips when it comes to mixing metals in every room.

MY NO-FAIL KITCHEN METAL COMBOS

Stainless steel and gold

Chrome and black

Satin brass and polished nickel

NO MORE THAN THREE

This rule applies especially in smaller rooms. In this case, try not to mix more than two metals. In larger rooms, such as a large living room or kitchen, you can use up to three. My biggest piece of advice would be to select one dominant metal to carry through the entire room. In other words, use mostly gold, then place the remaining metal colors selectively to create balance.

SELECT YOUR DOMINANT FINISH

When you are mixing metals, try to remember the 60:30:10 rule mentioned at the beginning of the Style Guide (page 142). For example, your dominant metal should be all over the room, such as in the cabinet knobs, pulls, door hinges, or doorknobs. The second metal (aka an accent metal) should be used for your plumbing and lighting. If you are using a third metal, such as stainless steel and black or gold finishes, carefully add it in through other accessory hardware.

AVOID LOOK-ALIKE METALS

Brass and gold are way too close in appearance and can clash when placed together in a room. Instead, aim for your two or three metals to look nearly opposite to each other. An example of this would be matte black and brass.

CATER TO YOUR AESTHETIC

If you are going for a warm aesthetic choose brass, gold, and copper. If you want a cooler aesthetic, go for nickel, stainless steel, and chrome finishes.

LIGHTING FIXTURES

ENTRYWAY

For smaller spaces, I mostly use a flush mount. If you want to put in a chandelier, find the right size for your large entryway using the following formula:

Room Length (in feet/meters) + Room Width (in feet/meters) = Chandelier in diameter (in inches/cm)

If you have a window at the front of your home, hang the chandelier centered in the window. If you are hanging one above an entryway staircase, ensure that you allow 84 to 90 inches (213 to 229 cm) of room under the light to give it proper space.

LIVING ROOM

In order to create a cozy atmosphere, we need to spread the light around the room at various heights (high, middle, and low). Remember, every room needs two to three light sources. I like to mix the room with table lamps, floor lamps, and wall sconces. Specifically, wall sconces create a warm and pretty glow without overwhelming the senses. The main goal here is to have your room well-lit so you can see what you are doing without having to strain your eyes. Apply the idea of task lighting. (See page 41.)

KITCHEN

For a simple all-white kitchen, select lighting that makes a grand statement. If the kitchen has lots of textures and patterns, pick a fixture that is more subtle to not overwhelm the senses. If a kitchen has a more modern vibe to it, choose a pendant with clean lines, geometric shapes, or organic textures such as rattan. If the kitchen is traditional, opt for pretty lantern-style pendants in historical brass metal.

DINING ROOM

We want our dining experiences to have an intimate vibe. My suggestion would be to install a dimmer switch. Dimmer switches are great because they allow you to be flexible with your lighting settings. Also, stay away from overhead lights. Instead, use various table lamps or floor lamps if space allows for it. This will create a beautiful ambiance.

BEDROOM

Table lamps on nightstands or standing lamps are most typical for bedrooms. Another option would be to add a crown jewel, a.k.a. a chandelier or ceiling fixture. With any ceiling light, your aim is to *not* hang it dead center of the room. Instead, try to center it above the room's largest feature: the bed.

BATHROOM

With your vanity, the best option is to use sconces mounted on both sides of the mirror. Light is delivered from different directions to illuminate your face. You will want to place the sconces within 2 to 3 feet (0.6 to 0.9 m) of each other. One common mistake people make is putting recessed lighting directly over their mirror. This causes the face to look darker and creates shadows. If you have a large enough bathroom, you can also add a statement chandelier.

HOME OFFICE

Always position your desk either against a window or next to a window. You never want to have your back to the window, or else you'll get an awful glare on your computer screen. Also add task lighting (page 41) with table lamps and standing lamps, or even wall sconces. Directly over your desk, you can even add a pendant or ceiling fixture.

LIGHTING HEIGHTS

KITCHEN PENDANT

The bottom of your pendants should hang anywhere between 34 to 36 inches (86 to 91 cm) above your kitchen island or countertop. If you have 8-foot (2.4 m) ceilings, your pendants will be closer to 30 inches (76 cm) above your island or countertop.

   If you have a longer kitchen island, install more pendants. You should have one light for every 2 feet (0.6 m) of kitchen island length. For a small kitchen island of around 4 feet (1.2 m), add two small pendants. If your island is between 5 to 7 feet (1.5 to 2 m), add two midsized pendants. If you have a large kitchen with a large island about 8 to 10 feet (2.4 to 3 m) long, consider three large pendants.

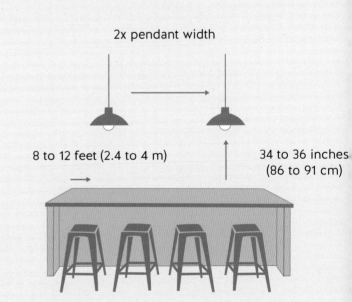

2x pendant width

8 to 12 feet (2.4 to 4 m)

34 to 36 inches (86 to 91 cm)

DINING ROOM CHANDELIER

Choose a chandelier that is half the width of the dining table. The ideal distance to hang a chandelier above the dining table is 30 to 34 inches (86 to 91 cm). This works with any type of dining room. If the chandelier is too high, it may not provide functional lighting for the eating area below. But a chandelier hung too low is tough on the eyes and may create a glare on the table. A chandelier hung at the correct height is a stunning focal point and draws the eye upward which enhances the perceived height of the room.

BEDROOM CHANDELIER

A chandelier over the bed can be hung 5 to 7 feet (1.5 to 2 m) above the floor. Unsure of what size chandelier you need? Pick one that is one-third of the size of your bed. The chandelier should complement, not overpower, the bed placed under it.

30 to 36 inches (86 to 91 cm)

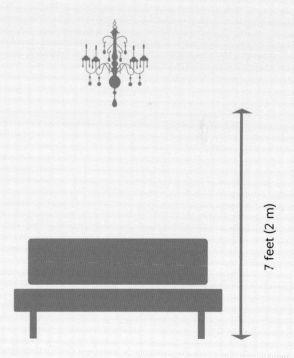

7 feet (2 m)

ROOM STYLING

There is no "one-size-fits-all solution" when it comes to styling a room. Our homes are all different shapes and sizes. To determine the best setup for you, first assess your needs. In other words, how do you live your life? Do you have children? Pets? Do you entertain often? Are you an organized person or a disorganized person? It's important to think through your life habits and space to figure out what you need and what you don't.

In the following section, I will offer you some advice to get started. You'll find my recommendations of items to buy, how much negative/walking space should be left, and even layout diagrams that have worked well for me when designing for a client.

LIVING ROOM LAYOUTS

The style of sofa you purchase for your living room will determine the size and shape of your coffee table. You can also buy multiple pieces of seating, such as chairs, love seats, and lounges. Before we get into the layout options, here are a few tips when it comes to styling your living room:

- **Sofa:** The distance from the sofa to the wall should be at least 12 inches (30 cm).

- **Coffee table:** The distance between the sofa and the coffee table should be about 16 to 18 inches (41 to 46 cm).

- **Chairs:** The distance between side-by-side chairs should be about 24 to 42 inches (61 to 107 cm). They should face the center of the room.

- **Negative space:** The walkway space should be 24 to 36 inches (61 to 91 cm) wide.

A standard sofa holds about three people and is usually in the shape of a rectangle. When choosing a coffee table make sure that it is one-half to two-thirds the length of the sofa.

STANDARD SOFA

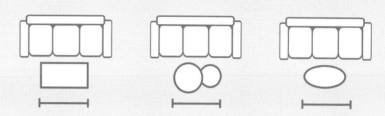

Also known as L-shaped couches, these seat at least five people with a long horizontal side and an attached chaise longue. For these couches, make sure your coffee table is one-half to two-thirds the length of the horizontal seat.

SOFA WITH A CHAISE LONGUE

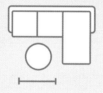 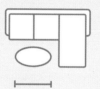 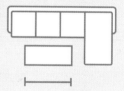

A large couch, these hold at least six people with two equal-sized sides. Make your coffee table one-half to two-thirds the length of one side.

CORNER SECTIONAL

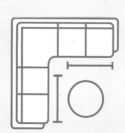 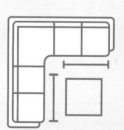

KITCHEN LAYOUTS

There are several kitchen layouts to choose from, and you and/or your contractor should decide what will be the best for you and your family. But first, here are a few tips when it comes to styling your kitchen:

- **Metals:** Select three metals at most, using the primary finishes for permanent fixtures such as lighting and secondary finishes for cabinet hardware.

- **Cabinets:** The best paint finish for kitchen cabinets are semigloss or gloss as they're great for high moisture areas and are very durable. You can save money by having them professionally spray-painted.

- **Countertops:** Marble easily absorbs stains but is tough to maintain and pricey. Instead, I suggest wooden butcher blocks to give warmth and character or granite because it's durable and less costly.

- **Appliances:** I recommend splurging on luxury appliances for the best quality and longevity.

- **Lighting:** A bright and bold fixture will make a huge impact.

- **Backsplash:** Many homeowners gravitate toward high-end tile backsplash, but you can also add beautiful color, dimension, and texture here.

KITCHEN WORK TRIANGLE AND GALLEY KITCHEN

The most successful kitchen layout creates an isosceles triangle between the stove, fridge, and sink, making the flow of movement when prepping meals and cleaning easier. The galley kitchen utilizes the work triangle. The kitchen is long and narrow with cabinets and countertop space located on one or both sides. It best suits two people.

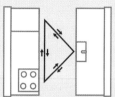

U-SHAPED

This layout is great for storage and best in a larger kitchen. If you use this layout in a smaller square foot kitchen, the space will feel crammed.

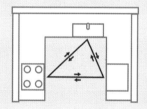

L-SHAPED

This layout is ideal for easy flow in corner kitchens. It can also be used in a small or large kitchen.

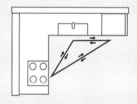

ISLAND

An island adds counter space and storage. Many island layouts utilize the L-shaped layout within it.

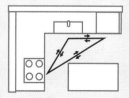

DINING ROOM LAYOUTS

Before getting into the layouts, here are a few tips for styling a dining room:

- **Table:** The size of your space will determine the size of your table. Choose between the shapes of a rectangle, square, circle, or oval.

- **Chairs:** Dining chairs do not have to match the table perfectly. Take two different styles, such as glam and rustic, and mix them together.

- **Art and gallery walls:** Artwork should be about two-thirds the length of your dining table. If you add art or mirrors above a buffet table against a wall, hang it 4 to 6 inches (10 to 15 cm) above the top of the table.

- **Texture:** Add texture with wicker Roman shades on the windows, velvet or patterned curtains, a metal chandelier, wood accents, or jute rugs.

- **Trim:** Crown molding is the perfect way to add interest to a room and draw the eye up. You can also add new baseboards.

- **Mantle:** For a bit of drama or a statement piece, a mantle is a great addition.

The formal dining room is an individual room of its own with the sole purpose of being used as a traditional dining room.

FORMAL

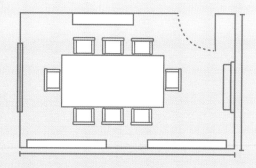

The pass-through dining room, while also a room on its own, has open doorways that allow you to pass from room to room.

PASS-THROUGH

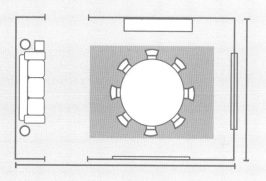

The informal dining room is an open space that may be shared with the living room and/or kitchen.

INFORMAL OR DUAL-PURPOSE

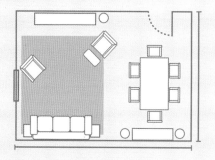

BEDROOM LAYOUTS

Bedrooms should be customized to the owner of the room, but there are still a few general tips everyone should follow before they choose the layout:

- **Bed:** Its placement depends on the size of the room and its occupancy.

- **Nightstands:** These should be level with the top of the mattress.

- **Lighting:** Overhead recessed lighting is not enough to light the bedroom. Always add two or three types of lighting within the room.

- **Vanity or desk:** If you have room to make a multipurpose bedroom, add a vanity table, with or without a mirror, against a wall.

- **Sofa:** If you have a large space, I always recommend adding a small conversation area with a small couch and table to give any empty space functionality.

STANDARD

A standard-sized bedroom is about 14 x 16 feet (4 x 5 m).

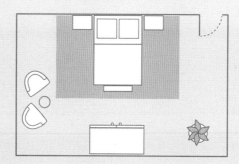

SMALL

A small bedroom is about 9 x 12 feet (3 x 4 m).

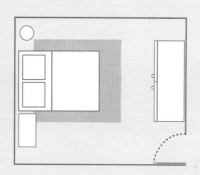

LARGE

A large bedroom is about 20 x 12 feet (6 x 4 m).

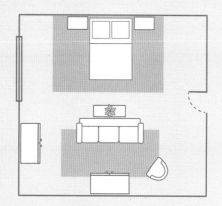

NURSERY LAYOUTS

Think about "zones" when putting together the nursery. For example, the sleeping zone, changing table zone, feeding zone, playing zone, and storage zone. Follow these tips for the furniture pieces you'll need and how to choose them:

- **Crib:** I always select the crib first.

- **Changing table:** If you choose to buy a dresser instead of a changing table, make sure you have safety features, such as straps and high sides, and a changing table topper.

- **Rocker or glider:** Having a cozy place to sit is crucial for bottle-feeding or nursing. Make sure to place it 2 to 3 feet (0.6 to 0.9 m) away from any wall so no bumping occurs.

- **Storage:** A dresser, small bookshelves, or tall bookshelves are great storage pieces. If you choose a taller bookshelf, I recommend adding safety furniture straps to secure it to the wall.

- **Blackout curtains:** Invest in blackout curtains so your baby can sleep peacefully no matter the time of day.

- **Carpet or rug:** If you can, invest in wall-to-wall carpeting for when the baby begins to crawl. Otherwise, choose a large plush rug.

If you don't have carpet in your nursery, rugs are a great substitute. Use a basic triangle layout of the crib, bed, and chair designed around the rug.

RUG SIZES

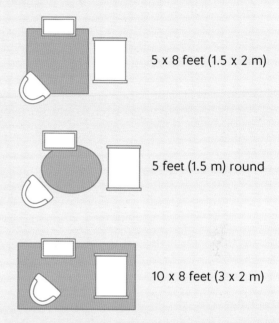

5 x 8 feet (1.5 x 2 m)

5 feet (1.5 m) round

10 x 8 feet (3 x 2 m)

If the baby's nursery is in a room that gets a lot of natural light, place the crib next to the window (not under it where the baby will feel cold drafts). By placing the crib next to the window, the sunlight will naturally glow past the crib without shining in a sleeping baby's eyes.

LAYOUTS

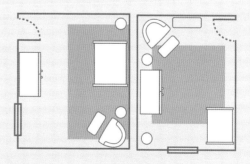

HOME OFFICE LAYOUTS

A home office can be its own room, a pass-through room, or a small nook transformed into a functioning space. Depending on your space, know these essential tips:

- **Desk:** This could be a corner desk or a long desk with lots of drawer storage. If you're working in a small space, try a narrow wall desk.

- **Chair:** A decent, cozy chair is crucial. For smaller spaces, invest in an acrylic or "ghost" chair.

- **Storage:** Storage options range from desktop organizers, desk drawer organizers, a wall of cabinets, secret storage for knickknacks, a storage ottoman, bookcases, and floating shelves.

- **Lighting:** *Never* place your back to the window when sitting at your desk. Opt for table lamps (I suggest one with an adjustable arm), standing lamps, or wall sconces.

- **Conversation area:** If you have the space, add a small sofa, a pair of chairs, and a small table for a conversation area.

STANDARD

10 feet (3 m)

10 feet (3 m)

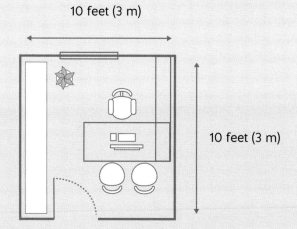

SMALL

10 feet (3 m)

7 feet (2 m)

9 feet (2.7 m)

8 feet (2.4 m)

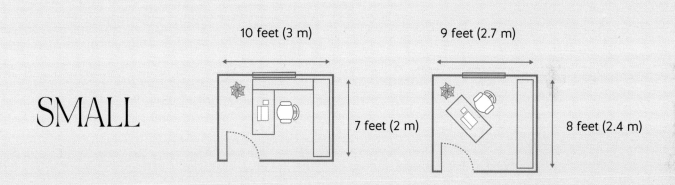

LARGE

9 feet (2.7 m)

12 feet (3.6 m)

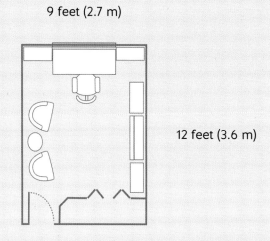

PAINT

Color affects your mood. With literally thousands of choices when it comes to choosing the right color for your home, things can get overwhelming fast! I have already discussed color schemes, but we have not yet discussed how paint can affect your overall mood as well as the paint finishes to choose from.

It's a scientific fact that color affects our moods. This is called "room color psychology." Certain colors in a room can provoke feelings such as zeal, happiness, and excitement. Overall, room color psychology affects your everyday life.

The colors you paint your home should reflect your unique personality. Homeowners make rooms unique by choosing colors that reflect their lives. You can pick color schemes or choose ones that simply make you happy (of course, you'll want some kind of coordination here, so don't go too crazy).

PAINT FINISHES

MATTE/FLAT

Great for rooms that do not get a lot of foot traffic because it's difficult to clean. Also great for ceilings.

EGGSHELL

With a slight sheen and low reflectivity, it is most popular for bedrooms, offices, and living rooms and it's easy to clean.

SATIN

A medium gloss that offers higher reflectivity than eggshell, use for areas of kids' rooms or hallways.

SEMIGLOSS

Water-resistant, this is a great choice for kitchens and bathrooms, as well as in window castings, baseboards, trims, and doors.

HIGH-GLOSS

This finish gives a dramatic yet beautiful impact on rooms and should be done by a professional. Durable and easy to clean, I recommend it for trims.

PAINT COLORS

Now let's dive into each color and the kind of moods they bring to a room. I've also listed my favorites to use to help narrow the decision process down a little bit more.

MOOD

VALERIE'S FAVORITES

RED

Red increases energy levels because it is intense! Associated with excitement and power, I would recommend using red paint in dining rooms because it's said to stimulate appetite. A home gym is also a great room to paint red. That being said, I would *not* use red in bedrooms as this color tends to raise the heart rate.

Benjamin Moore Moroccan Red

Sherwin-Williams Borscht

Farrow & Ball Rectory Red

	MOOD	VALERIE'S FAVORITES
YELLOW	Yellow evokes happiness. It is a sunshine color. Soft shades of yellow uplift the mood! It can also increase our focus. I love using yellow in bathrooms, home offices, family rooms, kitchens, and dining rooms.	Behr Candlelight Yellow Benjamin Moore Weston Flax Benjamin Moore Hawthorn Yellow
GREEN	Green evokes a calming mood and is associated with relieving stress, renewal, and nature. Since green is made from yellow and blue, it gives off calming and tranquil vibes. Use it in primary bedrooms, family rooms, kids' rooms, home offices, and bathrooms.	Benjamin Moore October Mist Benjamin Moore Windsor Green Benjamin Moore Tate Olive
BLUE	Blue is the most relaxing color and tends to lower blood pressure and evokes a sense of calm. It's associated with trust and stability. Use it in bedrooms, spas, home offices, and bathrooms.	Benjamin Moore Silver Gray Benjamin Moore Hale Navy Benjamin Moore Palladian Blue

MOOD	VALERIE'S FAVORITES

PURPLE

Purple evokes a mood of rich sophistication and contentment because of its darker shade. Lighter purple shades like violet and lavender give off a relaxed mood. Use it in bedrooms, kids' rooms, and bathrooms.

Benjamin Moore Misty Lilac

Benjamin Moore Sugarplum

Benjamin Moore Spring Lilac

PINK

Pink evokes a calming mood and is often associated with love and kindness. It is beautiful in bedrooms and nurseries.

Farrow & Ball Pink Ground

Farrow & Ball Rangwali

Benjamin Moore Melted Ice Cream

BROWN

Brown is a traditional beauty! This color is associated with warmth and elegance and evokes a cozy and safe mood. Use it in home offices, dining rooms, bedrooms, and mudrooms.

Behr Havana Coffee

Behr Dark Truffle

Farrow & Ball Tanners Brown

	MOOD	VALERIE'S FAVORITES

BLACK

Black evokes an edgy mood! It is best used in small doses as an accent. For example, black painted window trim is dramatic and beautiful. Black is also cool for a fireplace.

Farrow & Ball Off Black

Glidden Onyx Black

Valspar Dark Kettle Black

BEIGE

Beige is warm and homey. It's often used to warm up a room that may be considered "too cold," as it evokes a calm, dependable, and relaxing mood. It can be used in any room.

Glidden Fossil Stone

Behr Cotton Sheets

Valspar Cream in My Coffee

WHITE

White paint for walls is a timeless classic and can be used in traditional and modern homes. It evokes a calm mood and makes a room look open and large. Use it in any room!

Benjamin Moore White Dove

Benjamin Moore Swiss Coffee

Sherwin-Williams Alabaster

FURNITURE SHOPPING

Something to keep in mind when budgeting is choosing between high-end and low-end furniture. What is the difference between the two? What can you expect from each? Think about a less expensive sofa online that looks just like the more expensive version a designer showed you. While you can certainly find a cheaper version of a high-end piece, there are some downfalls to know.

WHEN TO BUY FAST FURNITURE

Many designers shy away from fast furniture stores because their products are usually made from lower quality materials such as softwood, plywood, pine, melamine, and laminates. While I'm not saying they are the worst places to shop for furniture, the lower the quality, the more likely they won't last very long.

I have used fast furniture in my own home for certain rooms. A rule to go by is to only purchase accessory furniture from fast furniture stores. A few instances include when you are furnishing a first apartment or a kid's room. Specific accessory pieces include end tables, kitchen stools, bedding, and wall décor.

WHEN TO BUY HIGH-END FURNITURE

It is true that low-end furniture is not as comfortable as high-end furniture. Better quality furniture is handcrafted by artisans who are experts in their craft. They use top stitching for sturdy seams that will not bust, strong materials, and hardwoods such as oak and mahogany.

Focal points, or furniture that will need to weather a lot of your downtime, should be comfortable and well made. Buying a well-made sofa or bed will save you money in the long run as a well-made traditional-style sofa can last up to a lifetime! You will also notice that pieces made from hardwoods are handed down from generation to generation. Other items you should buy at high-end stores are living room chairs and dining room furniture.

VALERIE'S FAVORITE STORES

As a designer, I have *many* places I source client products from. I love finding undiscovered companies. They are true gems that I get to keep in my back pocket, especially when it comes to amazing and unique design products.

   In the following sections, I will share some of my favorite companies and small stores that are for high- and low-end budgets. Just because you cannot spend a million bucks does not mean you cannot make your home look amazing.

FURNITURE

HIGH-END

"To trade only," which means that they are only available for designers, are: Kravet, Universal Furniture, Currey & Company, Ebanista, and Cassina.

   Luxury furniture stores are: Jayson Home, Perigold, RH (formerly Restoration Hardware), Rejuvenation, Lulu and Georgia, Serena and Lily, Arhaus, ABC Carpet & Home, Roche Bobois, and Ligne Roset.

BUDGET-FRIENDLY

My favorite low-end/affordable furniture stores are Wayfair, Target, Overstock, The Dump, IKEA, and Amazon.

   My favorite middle-priced stores are Pottery Barn, Crate & Barrel, CB2, Frontgate, and West Elm.

	HIGH-END	BUDGET-FRIENDLY
RUGS	One Kings Lane, Pottery Barn, Patterson Flynn, Locust Lane Rugs, Vermillion Rugs, Perigold, and Serena and Lily.	Rugs USA, Ballard Designs, Revival, Ruggable, Rugs.com, Etsy, Annie Selke, and Smallable for the kiddos.
LIGHTING	Visual Comfort & Co, Currey & Company, Ralph Lauren, The Urban Electric Company, Apparatus Studio, Kelly Wearstler, Schoolhouse, and Hudson Valley Lighting Group. For pendants and chandeliers, I recommend One Kings Lane, Lumens, Burke Décor, Perigold, and Bloomingdales.	Recently, I have found some incredible designer lighting brands at HomeSense for a fraction of the cost. Great floor and table lighting can be found at places like Target, HomeGoods, Build.com, Lamps Plus, Amazon, Crate & Barrel, and CB2.
WALLPAPER	Schumacher, Brunschwig & Fils, and Gucci.	Spoonflower, Rebel Walls, York Wallcoverings, Hovia, Deus Ex Gardenia, Anthropologie, Sian Zeng, and Artza & Co. (Some of these places are smaller-owned businesses and provide amazing designs of high quality.)

	HIGH-END	BUDGET-FRIENDLY
ART	High-end art can be found at local art galleries made by private artists. You can find them in your city and on art websites like Masterworks, Singulart, and Chairish.	One Kings Lane, Etsy, Minted, HomeSense, Perigold, Paper Craft World, Great Big Canvas, 1stDibs, Saatchi Art, and Artfinder. My personal all-time favorite local antique shops to buy original art from are Kelly Hopter Interiors, Valerie Leuchs, Taryn Wells Art, Alex Soffer Art, Susannah Carson, Amy Smith Art, Hapi Art, and Alexis Walter Art. The Etsy shops KristaKimStudio, and Linenandcloth make amazing art prints.
DECOR	One Kings Lane, Tom Dixon, Assouline, Taschen, Erin Gates Design, Wolf and Badger, Maisonette, Uncommon Goods, Alice Lane Home Collection, St. Frank, and Anacua House. If you are local to Virginia, check out Crème de la Crème, Baileywyck Antiques, Revival, Middleburg Antique Gallery, and Thrill of the Hunt, and Beckon Home.	Target, CB2, Crate & Barrel, IKEA, Anthropologie HomeGoods, and HomeSense are the places mostly everyone knows about. My favorite affordable places include Jayson Home, Bloomist, H&M Home, Zara Home. Some of my all-time favorite Etsy shops for home décor include AccentMarks and ShopLittleDesignCo for throw pillows, DhurrieWorld and IndianArtRugs for rugs, LynnChalk does great custom drapes and shades, and CruelMountain makes custom lampshades.

PART THREE

COMMON QUESTIONS

CONGRATULATIONS! That was a lot of information we just went over. I hope it gave you some insight into the world of interior design. It is truly a study for those of us who do this professionally, but that isn't to say a person who doesn't have an interior design degree can't create a beautiful and welcoming space. No one knows how to create your space except for you. With this book, you are just one step closer to getting everything you've wanted in your perfect home. In case you still have some questions, I have created this final section to answer them. Let's finish with my most asked questions for every room of the home.

Common Questions

I WANT TO ADD A STYLISH TILE TO MY ENTRYWAY AREA, BUT I AM AFRAID THE KIDS WILL SCUFF IT UP. WHAT DO YOU SUGGEST?

Porcelain tiles are the way to go for homes with children and pets. It's a forgiving material, cost friendly, and it's TOUGH! It will last a long time.

WHAT IS THE BEST PAINT FOR A SMALL ENTRYWAY?

Entryways tend to be busy areas and walls can get easily scuffed. Eggshell paint adds sheen and can be spot cleaned with mild cleaning solutions and a warm cloth.

WHAT ARE SMALL ORGANIZATIONAL OPTIONS FOR AN ENTRYWAY CLOSET?

I recommend a hanging cubby organizer for items such as hats, scarves, mittens, etc. If you have room, you can also add a hanging shoe organizer.

CAN I USE WALLPAPER FOR A SMALLER ENTRYWAY OR WILL IT MAKE THINGS LOOK TOO BUSY?

You can absolutely use wallpaper in smaller areas! (See My *Gone With the Wind* wallpaper on page 18.) Choose a wallpaper with texture. This adds another dimension to the wall, which can trick the eye and make it appear larger.

WOULD YOU RECOMMEND WORD ART SUCH AS A "WELCOME HOME" OR "HOME SWEET HOME" SIGN?

Never. However, it's your home, and you should do what makes you happy. As a designer though, I would not recommend it.

HOW CAN I MAKE AN ENTRYWAY ENTICING TO THE EYE?

For grand staircases, if you love modern design, I recommend striking metal and Lucite rails. If you love a traditional style, go for a lovely stair rug runner with a strong wooden banister.

For smaller entryways, use patterned tiles to make smaller areas look large. Stylish doors add fabulous character, such as glass doors, as they can create the illusion of more space and provide an opportunity to see inside the home.

HOW DO I STYLE AN ENTRYWAY TABLE?

First start with the focal point such as large art or a beautiful mirror usually in the center. I use odd numbers when adding items to tables. Also, select items of varying heights to give visual weight to the table. Use table lamps and vases with stems to create height. For smaller objects, use candles or photo frames.

HOW IS A FOYER DIFFERENT FROM AN ENTRYWAY?

A foyer and entryway are often used interchangeably, which can get confusing. These days, an entryway is usually less formal, whereas a foyer is considered more "grand." However, both terms can be used.

WHAT ARE SOME INEXPENSIVE WAYS TO UPGRADE MY ENTRY AND MAKE IT LOOK CLEAN?

Upgrade your welcome mat. Many homes with a run-down welcome mat make a negative impression. You can find some for great prices at Target, Amazon, and Etsy.

Also, go bold with paint such as on the front door. Paint is affordable and can be purchased at your local hardware store or Home Depot. I love the charm of glossy black doors. Bold-colored doors can also draw attention to an otherwise underwhelming or small space.

Common Questions

I AM ON A BUDGET. WHAT PIECE SHOULD I INVEST IN FOR MY LIVING SPACE?

Since these rooms see a lot of wear and tear, I would suggest investing in a well-made sofa. My advice is to choose the highest quality sofa for your budget and go for styles that will stand the test of time rather than trendy pieces.

WHY SHOULD I INVEST IN HIGH-QUALITY FURNITURE IF MY KIDS OR PETS WILL JUST JUMP ALL OVER IT?

High-quality sofas/armchairs are built to last. In other words, it will withstand wear and tear of kids and pet claws. (Refer back to Furniture Shopping on page 192.) High-quality sofas can last for decades so that you will not have to replace your sofa every couple of months or years! If they are also traditional styles, they won't look outdated.

WHAT IS THE BEST WAY TO FACTOR IN LIVING/FAMILY ROOM STORAGE?

A coffee table with drawers or an ottoman with a lid are great for storing blankets or toys. For a smaller space, use floor-to-ceiling shelving units for books and trinkets. Storage baskets are great for remote controls, toys, batteries, small throw pillows, and extra candles.

For books, you can add a beautiful stand-alone cabinet to create height and style, and functionality. Lastly, window seats are a beautiful way to integrate hidden storage if you have the space.

WHAT IS THE BEST WAY TO CONCEAL THE TV?

If it's within your budget, try a Samsung Frame TV which disguises itself as classical art. You can also put a TV inside of an armoire. The benefit of an armoire is that it's traditional and creates additional storage!

MY PARTNER WANTS A LARGE SOFA, BUT I'M AFRAID IT'S TOO BIG FOR THE SPACE. WHAT DO YOU SUGGEST?

If you're working without a designer, take the measurements of the sofa, then place easy to remove masking tape on the floor to get a visual of how large the sofa will be. Don't forget to consider space for end tables.

In many circumstances my clients are afraid of buying large accessories or furniture, so they end up with a bunch of small pieces which result in a disorganized and cluttered room. Do not be afraid to go big with pieces like a sofa. In most cases, overscale furnishing or art can make the room feel larger than it actually is.

IN AN OLDER HOME WITH LOW CEILINGS, WHAT KIND OF LIGHTING DO YOU RECOMMEND?

A flushmount. These are installed directly into the ceiling. They are perfect for homes with lower ceilings because they look stylish but do not compromise on space.

HOW CAN I KEEP UP WITH DESIGN TRENDS IF I AM ON A STRICT BUDGET?

The best way to keep your home updated with affordable décor is to use small accessories that don't break the bank. I love adding throw pillows because they freshen up the space immediately. You can also swap them out depending on the season. Buy a pillow insert from Walmart or Hobby Lobby and then buy a bunch of pillow covers.

HOW HIGH DOES MY END TABLE NEED TO BE?

The general rule is that end tables should be the same height or slightly lower than the arm of the sofa or chair they sit next to. This makes it easy to place drinks on them and also looks aesthetically pleasing due to the balance and scale.

Common Questions

THE KITCHEN

I WANT TO GO TRENDY IN MY KITCHEN, BUT I AM AFRAID IT WILL GO OUT OF STYLE IN A FEW YEARS. WHAT DO YOU SUGGEST?

Go for more traditional options with your major finishes such as countertops and cabinets because these are expensive to change out. Then, bring in the trendy elements with accessories such as barstools or lights that you can easily switch out without breaking the bank. Wayfair, Amazon, and HomeSense have great options for affordable lighting.

WHAT ARE YOUR THOUGHTS ON PEEL-AND-STICK BACKSPLASHES?

I think they are a great idea for renters and temporary solutions in your home. However, they are not durable in the long run and will not last against water and humidity.

WHAT ARE YOUR RECOMMENDATIONS FOR KITCHEN BACKSPLASH TILES?

I prefer larger backsplash tiles that create a more seamless look. Larger tiles, such as 12 x 24 inches (30 x 61 cm) or 24 x 24 inches (61 x 61 cm), are also easier to cut. Grease and dirt are harder to clean on smaller tiles, and they require more cutting, laying, and grouting. I also love natural stone as it's not only gorgeous but easy to clean when it's properly sealed.

I HAVE A TINY KITCHEN. WHAT ARE SOME WAYS TO MAXIMIZE MY SPACE?

I recommend installing extra-long upper cabinets with molding. The molding looks beautiful and draws the eye up creating the optical illusion of added height. You can also add cabinets above the fridge and a wall pot rack to free up cabinet space. Pot racks come in a variety of sizes and styles and are not only functional but also add a decorative element.

WHAT IS A HELPFUL TIP FOR A DIY KITCHEN ISLAND?

Remember the spacing of a kitchen island. The aisle should be wide enough otherwise things may be cramped when multiple people are in the kitchen. A general rule is to keep 42 to 48 inches (107 to 122 cm) of space between the island and countertops.

IS IT WORTH IT TO HIRE A DESIGNER TO HELP REDO MY KITCHEN?

Big YES! While a simple cabinet paint job can be an easy DIY, major remodels should be left to the professionals. Certain types of planning are involved such as moving possible electrical lines, gas lines, and plumbing. Designers can help you with efficient floor plans, find good lighting, appliances, and the best quality materials for your budget. They also have access to the best contractors and retailers in your local area. Designers and contractors also sometimes have trade discounts which can apply to anything from furniture to appliances.

SHOULD MY KITCHEN CABINETS GO TO THE TOP OF THE CEILING?

The decision is totally up to you. There is no right or wrong answer with this. Some homeowners choose to have their cabinets reach the ceiling due to their personal aesthetic. They also want longer cabinets with more storage options.

Historically, kitchen cabinets did not reach the ceiling because ceilings back then were not always perfectly leveled. If you want a more traditional look, keep space between your cabinets and ceiling. This option will also save you money.

Common Questions

WHAT IS YOUR MOST REQUESTED RENOVATION PROJECT WHEN IT COMES TO DINING ROOMS?

Popcorn ceilings! Homes built between the 1930s and 1990s frequently have popcorn ceilings. Popcorn ceilings are not only unattractive, but they can be hazardous. Before 1977, it was common for them to contain asbestos! Asbestos can cause issues such as lung disease and scarring of the lungs. They're also a huge dust trap, which is gross considering dust can potentially fall into your food. A sleek and smooth ceiling is the way to go.

WHAT IS A GOOD WAY TO MAKE MY DINING ROOM APPEAR LARGER?

Large mirrors reflect both natural light and light cast from your chandelier. For narrow and/or limited space, you can add a bench on one or both sides of the table. This tricks the eye into thinking the space is open and you won't have chairs creating obstacles in the walkway.

WHAT IS THE DIFFERENCE BETWEEN BUFFETS, SIDEBOARDS, AND CREDENZAS?

The easy answer is how the pieces are built. A sideboard does not have legs, can be bulky, and is meant to sit directly on your floor. They typically have drawers that are used for storing cutlery, candlesticks, napkin rings, and napkins. A buffet is similar to a sideboard except with legs and acts as a storage center for dishes. A credenza is typically longer and shorter than buffets and sideboards. They are great for holding beverages or extra dishes during a meal. Credenzas are also commonly flanked by cabinets in larger dining rooms.

IN AN OPEN CONCEPT HOME, WHAT IS THE BEST WAY TO TIE A KITCHEN AND DINING ROOM TOGETHER?

Pair matching or cohesive elements in the two areas such as metal tones, patterns, and materials. This way, the separate spaces will flow together and appear natural within the home.

WHERE CAN I GET UNIQUE AND BEAUTIFUL GLASSWARE AND PLATES FOR FORMAL DINNER PARTIES THAT NOT MANY PEOPLE KNOW ABOUT?

I love French history, and at the Palace of Versailles, they had the loveliest Marie Antionette plates by a company called Given based in France, but they take orders online. Their product line is handmade faience: a fine porous earthenware that is tine-glazed and then fired repeatedly.

Another favorite company of mine is the classical Villeroy and Boch. This is a German manufacturer of ceramics known for their delicate attention to detail. My all-time favorite pieces are their Audun collection in porcelain and their dinner plates that present nostalgic scenes from early French village farms.

IS IT A GOOD IDEA TO DO A MOODY STYLE FOR THE DINING ROOM?

I LOVE a moody dining room. The best way to make it moody is by using paints of deeper tones. My favorites are Sherwin-Williams Green Black and Gravel Grey, and Benjamin Moore Vintage Vogue.

Common Questions

MY NIGHTSTANDS ARE TOO SMALL FOR TABLE LAMPS. WHAT IS A GOOD LIGHT SOURCE FOR ME?

Try an arm sconce. Arm sconces don't only look chic, but they are flexible and perfect for reading in bed. They should be hung 30 to 36 inches (76 to 91 cm) above the top of the mattress. You can buy plug-in versions of arm sconces as well.

WHAT SIZE SHOULD A BENCH AT THE END OF MY BED BE?

The key is to buy a bench that is about three-fourths the length of the bed. You can also add two shorter stools; just remember to stick with the three-fourths rule.

DO I ABSOLUTELY NEED A HEADBOARD TO MAKE THE BEDROOM LOOK PUT TOGETHER?

There is no design requirement for a headboard, and there are several other ways you can fill this space. You can add large art for a focal point, floating shelves for extra storage, or some fun neon light sayings for an eclectic and interesting look. Check out Etsy for some great options.

I LOVE THE LOOK OF A WELL-MADE BED, BUT I CANNOT SEEM TO RECREATE IT IN MY BEDROOM. WHAT ARE YOUR TIPS?

The first step is to add a fitted and top sheet. Next, tuck a cozy duvet around your mattress snugly. Add a coverlet and two to three Euro sham pillows depending on the size of the bed. Add your sleeping pillows and, finally, your throw or lumbar pillows.

WHAT ARE THE BEST WHITE PAINT COLORS FOR A PRIMARY BEDROOM?

White Dove by Benjamin Moore: A clean and classic white, it is also tranquil and soothing.

Chantilly Lace by Benjamin Moore: This is a beautiful pure white without strong undertones and it looks great with warm and cool accents.

Dover White by Sherwin-Williams: This one has just a touch of yellow for warmth. It's classic, clean, and serene for a bedroom.

School House White by Farrow & Ball: This is a soft white reminiscent of white hues used in old schoolhouses. It's timeless and luxurious.

WHERE SHOULD THE PRIMARY BEDROOM BE LOCATED IN THE HOUSE? IS THERE A DESIGN RULE TO THIS?

There is no rule when it comes to this. However, if you are an early riser, you will want to choose an east-facing primary bedroom. If you are a late riser, then north- or west-facing rooms would be better for you. If you are designing a new build custom home, I'd place the bedroom near the back, whether it's on the lower or the top floor. This will be the most quiet and private location.

CAN A HOME HAVE MORE THAN ONE PRIMARY BEDROOM?

Yes, it is possible. In fact, it is now a growing trend to have a guest room, with an en suite bathroom, that is close to the size of the primary bedroom. With certain floor plans and homebuilders it adds resale value and is attractive to homebuyers.

WHAT ARE YOUR THOUGHTS ON WALL-TO-WALL CARPETING IN THE BEDROOM?

First, it is your home and you can do whatever makes your space feel cozy. However, there are some pros and cons to wall-to-wall carpeting you might want to consider.

The pros are that it will naturally absorb noise, making your bedroom quieter. Carpeting also adds warmth as it is a natural insulator, which is great for the winter months. Some carpets also cost less, which is why many builders install it over hardwood.

The cons are that carpets take in moisture and odors. If you smoke, for example, the carpet will absorb the smell.

HOW LARGE OR WIDE SHOULD ART ABOVE THE BED BE?

Wall art above any piece of furniture should span between 60 to 80 percent the width of the furniture.

Common Questions

IS IT WISE TO INSTALL WALLPAPER IN MY BATHROOM?

Yes, you can put wallpaper in your bathroom. Peel-and-stick wallpaper is ideal for high-moisture rooms because it's vinyl and has no paper content that will develop mold. However, do not add wallpaper where it will be exposed to lots of splashing such as above a tub.

HOW CAN I MAKE MY BATHROOM APPEAR LARGER TO THE EYE?

Depending on your budget, glass doors are beautiful, and you will be able to see every inch of your bathroom. Darker colors can make a huge impact on a tiny room. Last but not least, use smaller floor tiles. Smaller tiles will have more room to repeat, giving the illusion of a longer room.

WHERE CAN I BUY BATHROOM TILE FOR ANY BUDGET OTHER THAN HOME DEPOT OR LOWES?

The Tile Shop has over 140 locations nationwide. They sell anything from marble, limestone, travertine, ceramic, glossy, porcelain, and wood tile options. Another is Artistic Tile from New Jersey but they have authorized deals nationwide. They pride themselves on a full customer service experience that includes customization.

WOULD YOU RECOMMEND AN OPEN VANITY INSTEAD OF A VANITY WITH DOORS?

I love open vanities! Open shelving will create a clean view of your back wall. I would style the open shelves with folded crisp white towels and attractive bottles filled with lotions/soaps. I would avoid placing items such as toothpaste and hair dryers out in the open. Instead, use wicker baskets to hide them.

WHAT ARE SOME GOOD PLACES TO SHOP FOR ALL-IN-ONE BATHROOM NEEDS?

Ferguson has locations all over the country where you can see their updated products in person. They have a great selection of tubs, showerheads, lighting, and vanities. If you do not live near a Ferguson showroom, Home Depot is a great alternative.

HOW BIG DOES A PRIMARY BATHROOM NEED TO BE? IS THERE A RULE?

There is no specific size that a primary bathroom needs to be. The main goal is to design a space that is functional to your individual needs and how you use the bathroom on a daily basis. If you do not need a large space, by all means, do not stress about it. Just make sure you have all your essentials and design accordingly.

WHAT ARE SOME GENERAL BATHROOM MEASUREMENTS I SHOULD KNOW BEFORE I BEGIN A BATHROOM RENOVATION?

A towel bar should be 42 to 48 inches (107 to 122 cm) off of the ground.

A robe or towel hook should be about 70 inches (178 cm) off of the ground.

A toilet paper holder should be 26 inches (66 cm) off of the ground.

A towel ring or bar for hand drying should be 20 inches (51 cm) above the countertop.

A mirror should be 4 inches (10 cm) above the vanity countertop.

Common Questions

WHAT SHOULD I AVOID BUYING FOR A BABY OR KIDS' ROOM?

A changing table! We had a changing table when our second child was born, and we barely used it. Your kids will outgrow changing tables in a few short years. Instead, opt for a traditional-style dresser and changing table topper. Once they grow out of the changing table, they can still use the dresser.

WOULD YOU RECOMMEND WHITE BEDDING FOR KIDS' BEDROOMS OR SHOULD I MAKE THE BEDDING MORE EXCITING?

I am a huge fan of all-white bedding for easy laundering purposes especially in kids' bedrooms. You can add fun throw pillows and brightly colored blankets for that exciting factor.

WHAT IS THE BEST BIG KID BED ON THE MARKET RIGHT NOW?

At the moment, I am loving the Pottery Barn Findley Storage Bed. Kids' rooms are in constant need of additional places to put books, toys, and extra sheets. This bed features four large under-bed drawers for a clutter-free space.

WHAT ARE THE BEST PAINT COLORS FOR BABIES' AND CHILDREN'S ROOMS?

My favorites by Sherwin-Williams are: Pure White, White Raisin, Cool Beige, Wallflower, Kale Green, Indigo. I also love Farrow & Ball colors: Skimming Stone, Pink Ground, Middleton Pink, Breakfast Room Green.

WHAT ARE COOL PLACES TO GET KIDS', BEDROOM WALL DECALS THAT AREN'T CHEESY LOOKING?

There are plenty of amazing Etsy shops that will provide you with custom wall decals. They are also well made and one of a kind. Pottery Barn Kids is another option for large and tasteful decals.

WOULD YOU RECOMMEND SPLURGING ON EXPENSIVE STORAGE SOLUTIONS OR STICK TO OPTIONS FROM PLACES LIKE DOLLAR TREE?

This depends on your budget and how your kids play. Dollar store storage options are great for small toys like bath toys, small stuffed animals, and Legos. These are perfect for the "low-key" kid who won't destroy everything they touch. However, these simply do not last long and will need to be replaced at some point. Higher quality pieces are stronger and can withstand more wear and tear. If your kids play on the more rougher side, I'd go for these, and you won't have to replace them for a while.

WHAT IS A COOL WAY TO DISPLAY CHILDREN'S ARTWORK IN BEDROOMS WITHOUT IT LOOKING SLOPPY?

Instead of using thumbtacks or tape, I use chic-looking frames from places like Target, Home Goods, and local vintage shops. Place children's art pieces in these frames and create a mini gallery wall with the various frames. The result is fun and eclectic, and my kids were so proud to see their art displayed.

Another option is to get a large corkboard. This will give the overall room an organized look because the artwork is in one spot and not scattered about.

Common Questions

HOW DO I MAKE MY HOME OFFICE LOOK EXPENSIVE?

Avoid standard office lighting. Instead opt for wall sconces, bookshelf lighting, or pretty chandeliers. Add architectural details such as moldings and chair rails. I would also add in a few pieces of furniture with luxury upholstery. You can also add decent hardware by swapping out builder grade doorknobs and cabinet handles for matte black, chrome, or polished brass.

WHERE IS THE BEST PLACE TO BUY NICE-LOOKING OFFICE DOORS TO INSTALL FOR PEACE AND QUIET?

Right now, I am loving Rustica Doors, Anderson, Cantera Doors, and White Shanty. They offer a variety of styles from rustic to modern black sliding doors. You can also find doors that fit this need at The Home Depot and Lowes.

WHAT IS A SOOTHING COLOR TO PAINT MY HOME OFFICE?

As I talked about in the Paint section (page 188), it is a scientific fact that color affects mood. A wall painted with a low saturation, like blue and green, will be soothing. My suggestion is green paint such as Benjamin Moore Hollingsworth Green or Farrow & Ball Skylight.

MY OFFICE IS TOO SMALL FOR A PRINTER. WHAT DO YOU RECOMMEND?

Keep bulky items such as printers in another room. If you have a Wi-Fi connection, you should be able to print items from your office without any issues.

HOW MUCH DESK SPACE DO I NEED IN A HOME OFFICE?

It depends on the type of work you do and the overall size of the room. If you are in the type of field that requires you to sift through lots of paperwork, you will need a larger surface area for organizational purposes. If your work is strictly remote computer work, a smaller area should be sufficient. However, at the end of the day, think about how you need the desk to function and what styles you like.

WHAT'S A FUN WAY TO SAVE SPACE AND ALSO KEEP MY OFFICE FUNCTIONAL AND STYLISH?

I love to get creative and turn everyday home office pieces into a chic design element. For example, I recently had a project where a frame TV was installed as the homeowners monitor in the office. It looked awesome and saved a ton of much-needed space. I'd suggest seeing what you have that can be transformed like this.

WHAT IS THE BEST AND STYLISH WAY TO SOUNDPROOF MY HOME OFFICE?

Try a solid core door with a brass doorknob. Solid doors are wonderful because they are beautiful and work as sound barriers. Another option is to invest in acoustic noise prevention curtains. Check out the website acoustic-curtains.com.

References

BATHROOM

Remodeling by JLC. 2021. Hw.net. https://www.remodeling.hw.net/.

The Tile Shop. 2024. https://www.tileshop.com/.

DINING ROOM

Style by Emily Henderson. February 18, 2020. Emily Henderson. https://stylebyemilyhenderson.com/.

GENERAL DESIGN

1stDibs. 2024. https://www.1stdibs.com/.

3M. 2023. MMM-ext. https://www.3m.com/.

abc carpet & home. 2024. https://abchome.com/.

Accent Marks. 2024. https://www.etsy.com/shop/AccentMarks

Alex Soffer. https://www.alexsoffer.com/.

Alexis Walter Art. 2024. https://alexiswalter.com/.

Alfonso Marina. 2024. https://www.alfonsomarina.com/.

Alice Lane Home. 2024. https://alicelanehome.com/.

Amy Smith Art. 2022. https://www.amysmith.art/.

Anacua House. 2024. https://anacuahouse.com/.

Annie Selkie. 2024. https://annieselke.com/.

Anthropologie. 2024. https://www.anthropologie.com/.

Arhaus. 2024. https://www.arhaus.com/.

Arteriors. 2024. https://www.arteriorshome.com/.

Artfinder. 2024. https://www.artfinder.com/#/.

Assouline. 2024. https://www.assouline.com/.

Baileywyck Antiques. Dec. 3, 2022. https://baileywyckantiques.com/.

Ballard Designs. 2024. https://www.ballarddesigns.com/.

Beckon Home. 2020. https://www.beckonhome.com/.

Bernhardt. 2024. https://www.bernhardt.com/.

Bloomingdales. 2024. https://www.bloomingdales.com/.

Bloomist. 2024. https://bloomist.com/.

Build.com. 2000-2023. https://www.build.com/.

Burke Décor. 2024. https://www.burkedecor.com/.

Caracole. 2024. https://caracole.com/.

Cassina. 2024. https://www.cassina.com/ww/en.html

CB2. 2024. https://www.cb2.com/.

Century. 1999-2024. https://www.centuryfurniture.com/.

Chairish. 2024. https://www.chairish.com/.

CruelMountain Etsy Shop. 2024. https://www.etsy.com/shop/CruelMountain

Currey and Company. https://www.curreyandcompany.com/.

DhurrieWorld Etsy Shop. 2024. https://www.etsy.com/shop/DhurrieWorld

Ebanista. 2024. https://www.ebanista.com/.

Erin Gates Design. 2024. https://eringatesdesign.com/.

Ethan Allen. 2024. https://www.ethanallen.com/.

Etsy. 2024. https://www.etsy.com/.

Ferguson Showrooms. 2019. https://www.fergusonshowrooms.com/.

Four Hands. 2024. https://fourhands.com/.

Frontgate. 2024. https://www.frontgate.com/.

Great Big Canvas. 2002-2024. https://www.greatbigcanvas.com/.

Hapi Art. https://hapiart.com/.

H&M Home. 2022. https://www2.hm.com/en_us/home.html

Hickory Chair LLC. 2024. http://www.hickorychair.com/.

HomeGoods. 2024. https://www.homegoods.com/.

HomeSense. 2024. https://us.homesense.com/.

IKEA. 1999-2024. https://www.ikea.com/us/en/.

IndianArtRugs Etsy Shop. 2024. https://www.etsy.com/shop/IndianArtRugs.

Jayson Home. 2024. https://www.jaysonhome.com/.

Kelly Hopter Interiors. 2021. https://kellyhopterinteriors.com/.

Kravet, The Lee Jofa Collection. 2024. https://www.kravet.com/lee-jofa

Krista Kim Studio Etsy Shop. 2024. https://www.etsy.com/market/krista_kim_studio

Lee Industries. 2024. https://www.leeindustries.com/.

ligne roset. https://www.ligne-roset.com/us/.

Linenandcloth Etsy Shop. 2024. https://www.etsy.com/shop/Linenandcloth

Lulu and Georgia. 2024. https://www.luluandgeorgia.com/.

Lumens. 2023. https://www.lumens.com/.

LynnChalk Etsy Shop. 2024. https://www.etsy.com/shop/LynnChalk

Masterworks. 2024. https://www.masterworks.com/.

Middleburg Antique Gallery. 2023. https://www.middleburgantiquegallery.com/.

Minted. 2008-2024. https://www.minted.com/.

One Kings Lane. 2019. https://www.onekingslane.com/.

Overstock. 2024. https://overstock.bedbathandbeyond.com/.

Paper Craft World. 2024. https://papercraftworld.com/.

Perigol. 2002-2024 by Wayfair LLC. https://www.perigold.com/.

Pottery Barn. 2024. Williams-Sonoma. https://www.potterybarn.com/.

QVC. 1995-2024. https://www.qvc.com/.

Ralph Lauren. 2024. https://www.ralphlauren.com/home

Rejuvenation. 2024. https://www.rejuvenation.com/.

RH (formerly Restoration Hardware). 2024. https://rh.com/us/en/.

Roche-bobois. https://www.roche-bobois.com/en-US/.

RVA Design Group. 2024. https://rvadesigngroup.com/.

Saatchi Art. 2024. https://www.saatchiart.com/.

Schumacher. 2023. https://schumacher.com/.

Serena and Lily. 2024. https://www.serenaandlily.com/.

ShopLittleDesignCo Etsy Shop. 2024. https://www.etsy.com/shop/ShopLittleDesignCo

Singulart. 2024. https://www.singulart.com/en/.

St. Frank. 2021. https://www.stfrank.com/.

Susannah Carson. https://susannahcarson.com/.

Target. 2024. https://www.target.com/.

Taryn Wells Art. https://taryn-wells.com/.

Taschen. 2024. https://www.taschen.com/en/books/architecture-design/.

The Dump. 2024. https://www.thedump.com/.

The House of Scalamandré. 2020-2024. https://www.scalamandre.com/.

Tom Dixon. 2024. https://www.tomdixon.net/en_us

Uncommon Goods. 2024. https://www.uncommongoods.com/.

Valerie Leuchs. 2022. https://www.valerieleuchs.com/.

Visual Comfort. 2024. https://www.visualcomfort.com/.

Wayfair. 2016. https://www.wayfair.com/.

west elm. 2018. West Elm UK. https://www.westelm.com/.

Wolf and Badger. 2024. https://www.wolfandbadger.com/us/.

Zara Home. 2024. https://www.zarahome.com/us/.

KIDS' ROOM

Crate & Kids. 2024. Crate&Barrel. https://www.crateandbarrel.com/kids/.

Maisonette. 2024. https://www.maisonette.com/.

Smallable. 2024. https://www.smallable.com/en.

LIGHTING

Apparatus Studio. 2024. https://apparatusstudio.com/.

Hudson Valley Lighting Group. 2024. https://www.hvlgroup.com/.

Kelly Wearstler. 2024. https://www.kellywearstler.com/.

Lamps Plus. 2024. https://www.lampsplus.com/.

Schoolhouse. 2023. https://www.schoolhouse.com/.

The Urban Electric Company. 2024. https://www.urbanelectric.com/.

PAINT

Benjamin Moore & Co. 2024. https://www.benjaminmoore.com/en-us

Farrow & Ball. 2023. https://www.farrow-ball.com/us/.

Sherwin-Williams. 2024. https://www.sherwin-williams.com/.

RUGS

Locust Lane Rugs. 2024. https://locustlanerugs.com/.

Patterson Flynn. 2024. https://www.pattersonflynn.com/.

Revival. 2024. https://www.revivalrugs.com/.

Ruggable. April 21, 2023. https://ruggable.com/.

Rugs.com. 2024. https://rugs.com/.

Rugs USA. 1998-2024. https://www.rugsusa.com/.

Vermilion Rugs. https://vermilionrugs.com/.

VIRGINIA-BASED SHOPS

Thrill of the Hunt VA. 2024. https://www.visitrichmondva.com/listing/thrill-of-the-hunt/8637/.

WALLPAPER

Artza & Co. 2022. https://www.artza.ca/en.

Deus Ex Gardenia. 2024. https://deusexgardenia.com/en-us

etoffe. 2024. https://www.etoffe.com/us/.

Gucci. 2016-2022. https://www.gucci.com/us/en/ca/decor-lifestyle/gucci-decor/wallpaper-c-decor-wallpaper

Hovia. 2024. https://www.hovia.com/.

Rebel Walls. 2024. https://rebelwalls.com/.

Sian Zeng. 2021. https://www.sianzeng.com/en-us

Spoonflower. 2008-2024. https://www.spoonflower.com/.

York Wallcoverings. 2024. https://www.yorkwallcoverings.com/.

ACKNOWLEDGMENTS

What an amazing experience this has been writing my first design book. Thank you so much to Nicole James for believing in my book and making this dream a reality.

My husband and sons, Jonathan, Cole, and Brexton, for your incredible support through this process. The encouragement you provided for me was exactly what I needed. THANK YOU and love you all.

My incredible in-laws, Bill and Marilyn. Love you!

My amazing friends, Daniela and Sarah, who have encouraged me from the beginning.

ABOUT THE AUTHOR

Valerie Darden is a Virginia-based interior designer and author. She founded Brexton Cole Interiors in 2014 and has designed homes from Utah to New Jersey to South Carolina. Her design approach is a timeless traditional style mixed with elements of modern and eclectic pieces to draw the eye in. Her designs and commentary have been featured in numerous publications, including *The Pioneer Woman Magazine*, *Northern Virginia Magazine*, *The Cottage Journal Magazine*, *Southern Living*, *MSN*, *The Washingtonian*, *Better Home and Gardens*, *H3R Magazine*, *The Zoe Report*, *Apartment Therapy*, *The Spruce*, *My Domaine*, and *The Every Girl*.

Valerie was born and raised in New Jersey. She moved to Virginia in the early 2000s. In 2011, she met and married Jonathan Darden, and they have two sons, Cole and Brexton.

VERSAILLES
Gazette des atours de Marie-Antoinette

10 9 8 7 6 5 4 3 2 1

ISBN: 978-1-57715-427-3

Digital edition published in 2024
eISBN: 978-0-7603-8885-3

Library of Congress Control Number: 2024941284

Group Publisher: Rage Kindelsperger
Editorial Director: Erin Canning
Creative Director: Laura Drew
Managing Editor: Cara Donaldson
Acquiring Editor: Nicole James
Editors: Keyla Pizarro-Hernández and Katelynn Abraham
Interior Design: Louisa Maggio Design
Photography Stylist: Charlotte Safavi
Additional Photography: Valerie Darden, pages 2, 37, 87, 119

Printed in China